LEGAL TRAIL SERIES®

SECURITIES REGULATION

McLaren Legal Publishers

New York

LEGAL TRAIL SERIES®

SECURITIES REGULATION

Benjamin Silbert, Esq.
University of Richmond School of Law

ISBN-10: 0-9820734-9-6
ISBN-13: 978-0-9820734-9-0

Published by
McLaren Legal Publishers LLC
552 Broadway, 3rd Floor
New York, NY 10012

www.mclarenpublishing.com
Email: contact@mclarenpublishing.com

Printed in the United States of America

HOW TO USE THIS BOOK

This law school study aid is a non-keyed book. While it includes many of the key critical cases in the subject addressed, it is meant to provide an overall rigorous review of the topic indicated and convey key concepts and points of law for general study. For a keyed book linked to a specific casebook, please use our Legal Path Series® of keyed books.

"All of what you need, none of what you don't"

Our law school study guides give you exactly what you need to understand the key principles of the subject, including the sometimes elusive Black Letter law. We are not a replacement for an in depth legal analysis of the subject matter covered; however, we do present what is absolutely critical in a very concise format.

TABLE OF CONTENTS
Securities Regulation

SECURITIES REGULATION

I. INTRODUCTION

1. The Securities Markets

   Securities markets are where securities (stocks, bonds, etc.) are traded amongst investors. The best known markets in the United States are the New York Stock Exchange, American Stock Exchange, and NASDAQ. This market can be split into two main sections: the primary and secondary market. The primary market is where new issues are first offered; subsequent trading occurs in the secondary market.

2. State and Federal Laws

   Federal Law
   Securities regulation is largely governed by federal law, with the Securities Act of 1933 ("Securities Act") and Securities Exchange Act of 1934 ("Exchange Act") the two main sources of law.

   State Law
   Blue sky laws are state regulation of the offering and sale of securities. Blues sky laws are designed to protect the public from fraud. Issuers must register their offerings and provide financial details. Most blue sky laws provide private causes of action for private investors who have been injured by securities fraud.

3. The SEC

   The Securities and Exchange Commission (SEC) was created by Congress through the Securities Exchange Act in 1934. The SEC has the power to register, regulate, and oversee brokerage firms, transfer agents, and clearing agencies as well as the nation's securities self regulatory organizations (SROs). The various stock exchanges, such as the New York Stock Exchange and American Stock Exchange are SROs.

The SEC is composed of five commissioners appointed by the U.S. President and approved by the Senate.[1] The statutes administered by the SEC are designed to promote full public disclosure and to protect the investing public against fraudulent and manipulative practices in the securities markets. Generally, most issues of securities offered in interstate commerce must be registered with the SEC.

4. Sources of Security Law

Although the Securities Act and Exchange Act are the main sources of securities law, other law is derived from the Uniform Securities Act of 1956 (model for state security law), Securities Litigation Uniform Standards Act of 1998 (pre-empted certain class actions under state law), and the Investment Company Act of 1940 (governs investment advisors).

II. DEFINITION OF SECURITY

1. The Definition of "Security"

The Securities Act of 1933 and Securities & Exchange Act of 1934 provides an exhaustive list of what can be classified as a security, and can include any investment device including novel, uncommon, or irregular devices under the "investment K" language.

Debt & Equity Securities
Securities are generally classified as either debt or equity securities. Bonds, debentures, and banknotes are known as debt securities because the corporation borrows money from investors. The investor is the

---

[1] http://law.uc.edu/CCL/34Act/sec4.html

creditor and the corporation is the debtor. Stock is the most common type of equity security and gives the investor ownership in the corporation. Stock is issued to raise money (capital) to grow a business.

(a) Stock and Notes

Stock
A stock is an ownership stake in a corporation. Therefore, one who buys IBM stock is an owner of IBM and has certain rights. The two most common forms of stock are preferred and common. Common stock generally has the following characteristics: (i) the right to receive dividends, (ii) negotiability, (iii) ability to be pledged or hypothecated, (iv) voting rights in proportion to shares owned, and (v) capacity to appreciate in value

Preferred stock owners usually carry no voting rights, but are to be paid out dividends and upon liquidation preferred stock owners are paid before common stock holders. Additionally, preferred stock may be converted to common stock under certain circumstances.

Note
A note is an investment with a valuable return. Generally, when a note has a maturity over nine months, it is presumed to be a security. However, mortgages and consumer financing notes are excluded in the definition of a security.

(b) Financial Instruments

A financial instrument is a real or virtual document representing a legal agreement involving some sort of monetary value. It can be classified generally as equity based, representing ownership of the asset, or debt based, representing a loan made by an investor to the owner of the asset.

(c) Investment Contracts

An investment contract is a contract or scheme for the placing of capital or laying out of money in a way intended to secure income or profit from its employment. An investment contract for purposes of the Securities Act means a contract, transaction, or scheme where a person 1) **invests** his money in a 2) **common enterprise** and is led to 3) **expect profits** solely from 4) the **efforts of the promoter or a third party**, it being immaterial whether the shares in the enterprise are evidenced by formal certificates or by nominal interests in the physical assets employed in the enterprise.[2] The *Howey* test, used by the Supreme Court, is a substance over form test; one must look at the economic reality of the situation.

Securities law is not applicable when the purchaser is motivated by a desire to use or consume the item purchased rather than anticipation of receiving return on investment.

When looking at "solely from the efforts" of others, the critical inquiry is whether the efforts made by those other than the investor are undeniably significant ones, those essential managerial efforts which affect the failure or success of the enterprise.

The expectation of profits comes in two forms. The first is capital appreciation resulting from the development of the initial investment. The second is participation in earnings resulting from the use of investor's funds (i.e. dividends, other periodic payments, appreciation in value of investment).

---

[2] SEC v. W. J. Howey Co., 328 U.S. 293

(d) Exempt Securities

Securities exempt from the Securities or Exchange Act are addressed in Section 4 of the Securities Act and include government bonds, promissory notes, commercial paper, municipal bonds, and private placements. It may be advantageous to issue exempt securities because it is time consuming and expensive to register securities with the SEC.

Commercial paper is an unsecured, short-term debt instrument issued by a corporation, typically for the financing of short-term liabilities like accounts receivable. Maturities on commercial paper rarely range any longer than 270 days.[3]

A private placement enables a corporation to raise capital through the sale of securities to a relatively small number of investors. Private placements investors are usually large banks, mutual funds, insurance companies, and pension funds.[4]

III. THE SECURITIES ACT OF 1933: THE REGULATION OF PUBLIC OFFERINGS

1. 1933 Act Disclosure Requirements

The Securities Act of 1933 is largely concerned with the primary market and mandates the disclosure of material information to investors to prevent fraud. The primary market is the initial sale of securities to the public from a corporation. The Securities Act has two basic objectives—to provide investors with adequate and accurate material information concerning securities

---

[3] http://www.investopedia.com/terms/c/commercialpaper.asp

[4] http://www.investopedia.com/terms/p/privateplacement.asp

offered for sale and to prohibit fraudulent practices in the offer or sale of securities. Additionally, the sale of securities must meet interstate commerce requirements, which typically is not a problem.

2. The Registration Process

Section 5 of the Securities Act requires a public offering file a registration statement with the SEC. Absent an exemption (see below), all offers or sales of securities must be registered in accordance with Section 5 of the Securities Act.

Before registration statement is filed, there can be no offers to sell or offers to buy. After the registration statement has been filed, oral offers and some written offers are permitted. No sale of securities is allowed until registration statement becomes effective, and a prospectus has been delivered to the purchaser.

Prospectus
A prospectus is a formal legal document that provides details about an investment offering for sale to the public. A prospectus should contain the facts that an investor needs to make an informed investment decision. There is a preliminary and final prospectus for stocks and bonds. The preliminary prospectus is the first offering document provided by the issuer and includes most of the details of the business and transaction in question. Some lettering on the front cover is printed in red, which results in the use of the nickname "red herring" for this document. The final prospectus is printed after the deal has been made effective and can be offered for sale, and supersedes the preliminary prospectus (see "The Waiting Period" below).

3. The Operation of Section 5 of the Securities Act

    (a) The Pre-Filing Period

The Pre-Filing Period is the time before the registration statement has been filed with the SEC. It prohibits use of mail or any means of interstate commerce to offer to sell or offer to buy securities to be offered by issuer, underwriter, or dealer (§ 5(c))

Gun jumping is the illegal publication of information, statements, and publicity efforts made in advance of the initial public offering. The publication or publicity efforts are supposed to have the effect of conditioning the public mind or arousing public interest in the issuer or in its securities. Gun jumping results in liability under Section 12(a)(1) of the Securities Act.[5] The theory behind gun jumping is that investors should make decisions based on the full disclosure in the prospectus, not on the information disseminated by the company that has not been approved by the SEC. If a company is found guilty of gun jumping, the IPO will be delayed. [6]

EXEMPTIONS FOR ISSUERS AND AGENTS
Certain parties are exempt from any gun jumping liability. They include:

- Negotiations and agreements b/t issuer and underwriter in privity of contract with the issuer.
- Well-known seasoned issuers are exempt entirely from gun-jumping prohibitions of § 5(c) (**Rule 163**)
  - Legend must be included in written communications

---

[5] http://www.law.uc.edu/CCL/33Act/sec12.html

[6] http://www.investopedia.com/terms/g/gunjumping.asp

- Written comm. must be filed w/ SEC
- Applies only to the issuer[7]
- Communications made by or on behalf of the issuer made more than 30 days prior to the filing of the registration statement (**Rule 163A**)
  - Cannot reference offering
  - Only communications made by issuer or on its behalf are covered by safe harbor
  - Burden is on issuer to take reasonable steps to prevent circulation of communication in 30-day period
- Reporting issuers can continue to publish regularly released factual business information and forward-looking info without restrictions (**Rule 168**)
- Must be the same type of release and by same method as released in the ordinary course of business
- Non-reporting issuers may continue to publish regularly released factual business info; no forward looking info; consistent w/ past practice (**Rule 169**)
- Announcements of proposed public offering; disclose amount

---

[7] http://www.law.uc.edu/CCL/33ActRls/rule163.html

and type of security; manner and purpose of offering; not the anticipated offering price (**Rule 135**)

Exemptions for broker/dealers:
They may publish certain information about issuers in pre-filing period

- **Rule 137**—directed at broker/dealers who are not participating (not in privity of contract with issuer or underwriter); allows publication of research reports, recommendations, and opinions concerning securities "in the normal course of business"
- **Rule 138**—permits broker/dealers who will be participating to publish or distribute research reports confined specifically to issuer's non-convertible fixed income securities
- **Rule 139**—permits a broker/dealers participating in distribution to publish research reports concerning the issuer or any class of its securities

Issuer Classifications
The SEC treats security issuers differently. Issuers are categorized into the following groups:

1. Non-Reporting Issuer—an issuer that is not required to file reports pursuant to **§ 13 or 15(d)** of the Exchange Act (including voluntary filers)

2. Unseasoned Issuer—an issuer that is required to file Exchange Act reports, but does not satisfy the requirements for **Form S-3** for a primary offering of its sec.
3. Seasoned Issuer—qualifies to use **Form S-3** to register primary offerings of its common stock, but does not meet the well-known seasoned issuer criteria

    a. Generally, one who has timely filed Exchange Act reports for 12-month period and has a public float of at least $75 million. These stocks have high liquidity within the secondary market.

    b. Well-Known Seasoned Issuers represent the largest amt of capital raised and traded in the public markets. They are required to file reports in accordance w/ **§ 13(a)** or **§ 15(d)**. To qualify as a well known seasoned issuer, the corporation must have either worldwide common equity (i.e. common stock) market cap of more than $700 million or issued more than $1 billion of non-convertible securities other than common stock in last 3 years. Additionally, the issuer must meet the registration requirements of **Form S-3.** The issuer must be current and timely in its Exchange Act reporting obligations for previous 12-months. If the requirements are met, then issuer can use automatic shelf-registration.

Shelf Registration

Shelf registration is used if current market conditions are not favorable for a specific firm to issue a public offering. A corporation can fulfill SEC filing requirements beforehand and go to market quickly when conditions become more favorable. The corporation must still file the required annual and quarterly reports with the SEC (Rule 415).[8]

(b) The Waiting Period

The Waiting Period is the time after the registration statement is filed.

- a. NOTE: it is the *underwriter*, not the issuer, who wants to disseminate information to gauge pre-sale interest—the rules allow the underwriter to distribute a free writing, which is in effect a summary of what the issuer has already filed in the registration statement (called the preliminary prospectus or "red herring")
- b. Section 5(c) not applicable; no prohibition against oral offers; only written; but, sales still barred under Section 5(a).
- c. Written offers may be made by means of Section 10(b) prospectus (free writing, below) as well as a Rule 134 or tombstone ad in accordance with Section 5(b)(1) prior to the effective date of the registration statement.
- d. The preliminary prospectus includes all of the information required by Section 10(a) of the Securities Act except for matters dependent on the offering price (Rule 430).

  Rule 430A—allows final pricing information to update the Rule 430 prospectus converting to § 10(a) final prospectus

---

e. The free writing prospectus is any written communication that constitutes an offer to sell or a solicitation of an offer to buy the securities relating to a registered offering and that is used after the registration statement is filed. It does not have to contain the same information as any other type of prospectus (not part of registration statement) (Rule 405).

- May contain information not set forth in the registration statement but must not conflict with such registration statement
- Rule 163: well-known seasoned issuers may use free writing prospectuses during any phase of an offering without violating Section 5 of the Securities Act
- Eligible seasoned issuers may use free writing prospectus only if registration statement containing a preliminary statutory prospectus has been filed
- Rule 164: eligible non-reporting issuers and eligible unseasoned issuers may use free writing prospectus if registration statement has been filed w/ the SEC and free writing is accompanied or preceded by the most recent statutory prospectus
- Ineligible issuers also may use free writing prospectuses during the waiting and post-effective periods but may provide only a description of

the terms of the offering and the securities offered
- The free writing prospectus is subject to Section 12(a)(2) disclosure liability and Section 10(b) anti-fraud provisions

f. Summary Prospectus—includes the information specified in the instructions as to summary prospectuses in the registration statement used by the issuer (i.e. Form S-3 includes instructions which specify info that must be included in a summary prospectus used by an S-3 filer)

g. Tombstone Ad
- An ad that qualifies for the Section 2(a)(10) exemption from the definition of a prospectus

h. Identifying Statement (Rule 134)
- Issuer may release general information about its business, terms of securities being offered, underwriters of the offering, details of the offering process, anticipated schedule of offering, description of marketing events, indications of interest and conditional offers to buy, and security rating expected.
- Availability of rule contingent upon the issuer filing registration statement
- Essentially, its an expanded version of a tombstone ad

i. Road Shows

- A road show is a presentation by the issuer of securities intended to create interest in the securities. It is often by the management of the corporation and is presented to analysts, fund manager or potential investors.
- A road show does not constitute a Section 2(a)(10) prospectus

j. Other Media

- Where information about an issuer or an offering is provided by the issuer or any participant and the information is subsequently published and constitutes an offer to sell, it will be considered a free writing prospectus
- Communications allowed, but issuer is required to file with the SEC such written communications within four business days of publication
- Non-reporting issuers and reporting seasoned issuers that have prepared or paid for media must precede or accompany communication with a statutory prospectus and file the media with the SEC
- A seasoned issuer that prepared or paid for media needs to have filed a registration statement with the SEC and file the media piece

- Well-known seasoned issuer may use media piece at any time, subject to filing the free writing prospectus with the SEC

k. Acceleration
- A registration statement becomes effective the 20th day after filing with the SEC; filing of an amendment commences the waiting period anew
- Section 8(a) gives SEC the power of acceleration so that it can determine to have the registration statement become effective immediately after the last amendment is filed

(c) The Post Effective Period
After registration becomes effective sales can be made.
a. Contents of final prospectus specified in Section 10(a) of the Securities Act
b. Final prospectus must be provided to or accessible to purchasers
- Access equals delivery— investors presumed to have access when final prospectus posted on internet (Rule 172)

4. Exemptions from Registration Under the 1933 Act

Under the Securities Act two types of exemptions exist: transactional exemptions & securities exempt from registration.

The securities exemption covers specific securities or categories that never require registration because of nature of issuer or security (i.e. promissory notes, municipal bonds, etc.)

A transactional exemptions means that for each separate transaction an exemption from registration must be perfected. The relevant parties are primary issuers of securities. The party seeking exemption has the burden of proving that it has perfected the exemption by establishing that it has satisfied the necessary conditions for invoking the exemption.

Failure to register gives rise to SEC or perhaps criminal liability. There is also private recover under Section 12(a)(1).

However, an issuer can make a rescission offer that fully informs purchasers of material facts and provides them with a right to rescind. Additionally, an issuer can seek an SEC no-action letter to determine whether enforcement action would be taken if contemplated conduct were undertaken in accordance with a written request.

(a) Private Placements

Section § 4(2) of the Securities Act is the private offering exemption which excludes from registration transactions by an issuer not involving a public offering. Exemption is self-determining w/ the burden of proof being placed on the issuer and other relying on the exemption

KEY FACTOR: availability of information to offeree (some say it's the only factor). Availability of exemption should turn upon whether the particular class of persons affected needs the protection of the Securities Act. The Securities Act requires that all persons to whom offers are made are provided with or have access to the type of information that would be contained in a registration statement.

(b) Small Offerings

See Regulation D and Regulation A below.

(c) Regulation D

Under the Safe Harbor Rules under Section 3(b) of the Securities Act, the SEC is authorized to exempt from registration securities if it believes registration is not necessary for the public interest or protection of investors.

1. Regulation D encompasses Rules 501-506[9]
   a. Rules 501-503 set definitions, terms, conditions, etc. that apply generally
   b. Rules 504-505 are specific exemptions from registration under Section 3(b)
   c. Rule 506 relates to transactions deemed to be exempt under Section 4(2)

2. **Rule 501**
   Rule 501 covers accredited investor. Accredited investors are institutional investors, private business development companies, tax exempt orgs, directors, officers, and general partners, $150K purchasers if not exceeding 20% of individuals net worth, individuals with net worth over $1 million, and individuals with $200K + income in last 2 yrs ($300K with a spouse) who expect the same income in the current year.

3. **Rule 506**
   a. Available to any issuer
   b. No limit to the aggregate price of securities offered

---

[9] http://www.law.uc.edu/CCL/33ActRls/regD.html

    c. No advertising or general solicitation is permitted

    d. Number of non-accredited purchasers is limited to 35 plus an unlimited number of accredited investors

- If any purchasers are non-accredited, then specific disclosures must be made to all non-accredited purchasers
- Suitability determination must be made for all non-accredited purchasers

    e. Issuer must take certain actions to guard against resale

    f. NOTE: The Section 4(2) exemption of the Securities Act may be a better alternative when non-accredited investors purchase because Rule 506 requires disclosure of information to all non-accredited purchasers whereas Section 4(2) allows offeree's access to information as a substitute for providing information.

4. **Rule 504**—blanket federal exemption from registration for offerings not exceeding $1 million

    a. Issuer need not determine whether purchaser is sophisticated

    b. Issuer need not provide representative for unsophisticated

    c. No limit on the number of offerees and purchasers

    d. Offerings limited to $1 million for any 12-month period

    e. General solicitation permitted and securities freely transferable

- Transactions must be registered under state law or exempt from registration under state law

5. **Rule 505**—provides any issuer that is not an investment company with exemption from registration

   a. Not more than 35 non-accredited purchasers; unlimited number of accredited investors
   b. May raise up to $5 million during any 12-month period
   c. General solicitations and advertising prohibited
   d. <u>Restrictions on resale</u>: Must provide written disclosure regarding limitations on resale to non-accredited purchasers
   e. Substantial compliance standard applies
   f. Must disclose certain specified information to purchasers
   g. No determination required as to whether purchaser is sophisticated; no requirement that investor has purchaser rep
   h. Exemption unavailable to issuers that have engaged in certain misconduct ("bad boy disqualifiers")

6. **Rule 508**—Substantial Compliance
   a. For offerings pursuant to Rule 504-506 exemptions
   b. Timely filing of a Form D with the SEC is not precondition for perfecting a Regulation D exemption; still must file Form D
   c. Rule 508 – defendant must show particular requirement not intended to specifically protect the complainant. It must be a compliance defect not

significant to offering as a whole and good faith reasonable efforts to adhere to all of Regulation D's mandates

EXCEPTIONS: substantial compliance defense cannot be invoked if it is a general solicitation; dollar limits in 504-505 offering are violated or number of non-accredited purchasers in 505-506 is exceeded

7. **Rule 502(c)**—Is a communication a general solicitation or advertisement?
   a. Is there a pre-existing relationship?
      i. Aids issuer in evaluating investor suitability
      ii. Substantive pre-existing relationship may be established by showing that subject party was aware of potential investor's financial circumstances or sophistication because either the investor had previously invested with the broker/dealer and the relationship had existed for an appreciable time period, or the investor had been effectively pre-screened.

   b. Has sufficient time elapsed b/t the pre-qualification of the potential investor and the participation by the issuer or its agents in the particular offering under consideration?

   If yes, is it being used by someone on the issuer's behalf to offer or sell the securities?

- By the issuer or someone on the issuer's behalf
- To offer or sell securities

    c. If either can be answered "no" then there is no violation

(d) Intrastate Offerings

<u>Section 3(a)(11)—Intrastate Offerings</u>
Any security which is offered and sold only to persons resident within a single state, where issuer of security is a resident and doing business within the state, is exempt from registering the transaction. Because no interstate commerce is involved, it is not within the jurisdiction of the SEC. An intrastate offering is less expensive than registering the SEC. Note that one non-resident sale invalidates the offering as does resale by residents to non-residents.

(e) Regulation A

Under Section 3(b) of the Act, Regulation A enables small companies with small offerings the ability to go public. The aggregate offering price for a Regulation A offering may not exceed $5 million. If the offering is made by or includes selling security holders, the maximum permitted by those selling security holders is $ 1.5 million. In either case, the maximum permitted is based on the offering price of all securities sold pursuant to Regulation A within 12 months before the start of and during the offering. Regulation A places no qualifications on offerees and purchaser, and securities offered and sold under Regulation A may be freely traded in the aftermarket.

(f) Mergers and Reorganizations

A merger is the combination of two or more companies, generally by offering the stockholders of one company securities in the acquiring company in exchange for the surrender of their stock.[10] Section 3(a)(10) of the Securities Act provides an exemption from registration for securities that are issued in exchange for outstanding securities, claims (including legal fees) or other property, or partly in such exchange, provided that a court or authorized governmental authority has approved the transaction on the basis of a suitable fairness hearing.

(g) Sales by Persons other than the Issuer

Securities Act Section 4(1) exemption from Section 5 registration requirements permits individual investors to resell their securities without registration provided such resales are viewed as transactions and not a distribution and such persons are not deemed underwriters.

(h) Problems Common to 1933 Act Exemptions

Exemptions are available when certain specified conditions are met. These conditions include the prior filing of a notification with the appropriate SEC regional office and the use of an offering circular containing certain basic information in the sale of the securities. Supplementary reporting rules adopted by the SEC in November 1998 require even exempt equities offerings to file reports with the SEC within the quarter following their issuance.

Potential Problems. SEC standards developed in 1997 and put in force in 1998 also relieve certain

---

[10] http://www.investopedia.com/terms/m/merger.asp

responsibilities formerly faced by large securities issuers under the original provisions of the act. These new regulations require large securities issuers to register with the SEC as always, but no longer require the mailing of a prospectus to potential investors. Instead, securities issuers may mail a greatly abbreviated prospectus to potential investors, while merely exhibiting the more exhaustive information online at the website of the SEC.

Despite the stringent registration requirements imposed by the 1933 Act, most US securities are not sold through public, registered offerings. Instead, one or more exemptions are used. The exemptions are non-exclusive, meaning more than one may apply to any given offering. Under Section 4(2), private placements may be made to institutions or other "accredited investors" deemed to be able to "fend for themselves" without a full registration. Regulation D codifies this statutory principal and offers more clearly defined safe harbor rules for those seeking a private placement exemption. Section 3(a)(11) offers the little used exemption allowing issues made only within one state to avoid registration. Rule 147 creates a clearly defined safe harbor for intrastate offerings.

Of greater importance, Section 4(1) allows for secondary market transactions to take place without registration - an essential provision allowing for market liquidity. Rule 144 allows company affiliates (insiders and control persons) and other owners of restricted securities to sell in some circumstances, and is discussed in detail below.

Rule 144A exempts resales of restricted securities between "Qualified Institutional Buyers," or "QIBs." This creates a secondary market in restricted securities among the biggest players on Wall Street. Note that Rules 144 and 144A accomplish different objectives.

Regardless of whether the securities are exempt from registration, antifraud provisions apply to all sales of securities involving interstate commerce or the U.S. postal system.

5. Civil Liability for Misstatements

    (a) Introduction (Elements of a 1933 Act sec. 11 Claim)

    Section 11(a) of the Securities Act specifies the classes of persons who may be subject to liability for material misstatements or omissions contained in the registration statement (or statutory prospectus).

    A. <u>Parties Subject to Section 11 Liability includes</u>:
        1. All persons who sign the registration statement
        2. Every director or general partner of the issuer
        3. Every person named with his/her consent in the registration statement as being or about to become a director or general partner of the issuer
        4. Every expert who has with his consent been named as having prepared or certified any part of the registration statement, or as having prepared or certified any report or valuation which is used in connection with the registration statement with respect to the statement in such registration statement, report, or valuation which purports to have been prepared or certified by him
        5. Every underwriter of the offering

6. Pursuant to Section 15, every control person of a party liable under Section 11
7. **EXCEPTION**: no aiding and abetting liability imposed under Section 11

B. <u>Elements of a Section 11 Right of Action</u>
   1. Must meet interstate commerce requirements
   2. A private right of action for damages may be brought
   3. By any person acquiring such security unless it can be shown that, at the time of purchase, the purchaser knew of the misstatement or omission
   4. Privity between the purchaser and the defendant is not required for recovery
   5. Section 11 right of action available at initial offering and for subsequent sales
   6. Plaintiff must show not only that he might have purchased shares by means of a deficient registration statement in a particular offering, but that he in fact did purchase such shares pursuant to that specific offering (must have standing)
   7. No reliance upon misstatement or omission necessary
   8. **EXCEPTION**: where the plaintiff acquired securities more than 12 months after the effective date of registration statement and issuer has made generally available earnings statement covering this 12 mo period, the plaintiff must prove reliance
   9. No need to prove that the material misrepresentation or nondisclosure "caused" the loss
   10. EXCEPTION: case law reduces plaintiff's monetary award by showing that loss was attributable to factors other than material misrepresentation in registration statement

11. Action must be brought within 1 year after the discovery of the untrue statement, or after such discovery should have been made by the exercise of reasonable diligence, but never more than 3 years after security offered to public

C. Defenses for Issuer
Generally, issuer is held strictly liable. An exception exits if the plaintiff knew of the misstatement or omission, lack of materiality of misstatement or omission, lack of causation, or expiration of statute of limitations.

D. Defenses for Non-Issuer
1. If non-issuer defendant discovers misstatement or omission, liability may be avoided by:
    a. Before the effective date of the registration statement, resigns from or takes such steps by law to resign from, or ceases or refuses to act in, any capacity or relationship to the registration statement, and advises the SEC and the issuer in writing of the action taken and disavowing responsibility for such part of the registration statement
    b. After registration statement becomes effective, if unaware that it had become effective and upon becoming aware of such fact: advises the SEC in writing and gives reasonable public notice that such part of the registration statement had become effective without his knowledge

2. Due Diligence (§ 11(b)(3))
    a. Due diligence is a defense and not an affirmative obligation

b. Unexpertised Portion – the defendant must show that, after reasonable investigation he had reason to believe and did believe at the time such part of the registration statement became effective that there was no material misstatement or omission

c. Expertised Portion - the defendant need show only that he had no reasonable ground to believe and did not believe that the expertised portion of the registration statement was defective

    i. Non-expert has no affirmative duty to make an investigation, but also must have no reasonable ground to believe that info is inaccurate

    ii. Expert is required to show that after reasonable investigation, he had reasonable ground to believe and did believe his expertised statement to be accurate

d. Due Diligence Standard (§ 11(c))

    i. Standard of reasonableness by which the concept of reasonable investigation is to be measured is that required of a prudent man in the management of his own property

    Applies to reasonableness of one's investigation and reasonableness of one's belief

    ii. Factors to be considered in determining reasonable investigation (Rule 176)—type of issuer; type of security; type of person; office held when the person is an officer; presence or absence of another relationship to the issuer when the person is a director or proposed director; reasonable reliance on officers, employees, and others whose duties should have given them knowledge of the particular facts; when underwriter, the type of underwriting arrangement and role of the particular person as an underwriter as well as availability of info with respect to registrant; whether, with respect to a fact or document incorporated by reference, the particular person had any responsibility for the fact or document at the time of the filing from which it was incorporated

(b) Persons Liable

Parties' Due Diligence Defense

a. Directors—distinction between inside and outside directors and based upon extent of knowledge of or access to pertinent facts
- Less is required of outside directors, but reasonable investigation still requires affirmative action
- Outside directors must make some independent verification of information contained in reg statement

b. Signatories—persons who sign
    registration statement may be held to
    stringent due diligence obligations
    - Inside signatories are in
      effect guarantors of the
      accuracy of the
      registration statement

c. Attorneys—one who renders legal
    advice or assists in the preparation of
    registration statement does not
    become an expert
    - EXCEPTION: counsel who
      renders a formal legal
      opinion in the registration
      statement is considered
      an expert

d. Underwriters—must make an
    independent verification of
    management representations and is
    expected to exercise a high degree of
    care in its investigation
e. Accountants—information obtained by
    accountants must be independently
    verified. Accountants are not held to a
    higher standard than that required of
    the profession.

(c) Liability under 1933 Act. Sec. 12
    Section 12 of the Securities Act addresses
    civil liabilities arising in connection with
    prospectuses and communications, and is
    divided in two parts.
    a. Section 12(a)(1) provides a
        purchaser of securities w/ an
        express private right of action
        against seller if seller offers or
        sells a security in violation of § 5

i. Purchaser may seek rescission, or if security no longer owned, damages

ii. Who is a seller? *(Pinter v. Dahl)*

    1. Encompasses those persons who successfully solicit the purchase, motivated at least in part by a desire to serve his own financial interests or those of the securities owner

    2. Liability imposed only on the immediate seller

    3. Includes:

        a. One who owned the security sold to the purchaser

        b. An agent for the vendor who successfully solicited the purchase

        c. One who solicited the purchase w/ the intent to personally benefit

        d. One who w/out financial benefit to oneself solicited the

purchase w/ the motivation to serve the owners financial interests

    iii. Liability may be invoked only by purchasers in registered offerings under the Securities Act and maybe by exempt offerings of a public nature (i.e. Rule 504)

b. Section 12(a)(2) gives express right of action to a purchaser against seller for rescission or damages if securities have disposed of, where purchaser acquired securities by means of a prospectus or oral communication which contained a material misstatement or omission

    i. Proof of reliance is not required (plaintiff need not prove he ever received prospectus)

    ii. Provides a reasonable care defense that may be similar to Section 11's due diligence defense

        1. Differences between Section 12(a)(2) and Section 11: Section 11 applies to registered offerings, Section 12(a)(2) remedy is limited to purchasers of securities in a public offering by an issuer or its controlling SH's. Therefore, Section 12(a)(2) extends liability only to those who sold the securities to the allegedly aggrieved purchasers

        2. The defendant can avoid liability by showing that he did not know, and in the exercise of reasonable care could not have known of the material misstatement or omission

iii. NOTE: liability based on information provided at time of sale, not time of effectiveness (Rule 159)

c. Controlling Person Liability

Section 15 imposes joint and several liability on any person who controls a person liable under Section 11 or 12 unless the controlling person had no knowledge of or reasonable grounds to believe in the existence of the facts by reason of which the liability of the controlled person is alleged to exist

> **EXCEPTION**: controlling person acted in good faith and did not directly or indirectly induce the act or acts constituting the violation or cause of action

IV. THE SECURITIES ACT OF 1934: THE REGULATION OF PUBLICLY-HELD COMPANIES

1. Overview of the 1934 Act

Unlike the Securities Act of 1933 which regulates the original issue of securities, the Securities and Exchange Act of 1934 is concerned with the secondary market. The Exchange Act of 1934 created the Securities and Exchange Commission (SEC). All stocks listed on stock exchanges must meet the requirements of the Exchange Act.

2. Periodic Disclosure Requirements

Under the Exchange Act, periodic reporting is used to satisfy much of the disclosure necessary in Securities Act registration statements. Some of the major disclosure requirements are as follows. Domestic issuers (other than small business issuers) must submit annual reports on Form 10-K, quarterly reports on Form 10-Q, and current reports on Form 8-K for a number of specified events and must comply with a variety of other disclosure requirements.[11]

Annual Report – 10K

Subject to Section 13 or 15(d), issuers of securities are required to file an annual report on Form 10-K. The 10-K provides a comprehensive overview of the company's business and financial condition and includes audited financial statements.

The essential content of the basic information package includes (1) audited financial statements, (2) a summary of selected financial data appropriate for trend analysis, and (3) a meaningful description of the registrant's business and financial condition.

A 10-K has to be filed with the SEC a certain number of days after the end of the company's fiscal year. The length of time depends on how much public stock or public float the corporation has. The biggest corporations, those with more than $700 million in public float, have 60 days to file with the SEC. Smaller corporations can have either 70 or 90 to file. A 10-K is now structured in four parts, to segregate the basic package.[12]

10-Q
The Form 10-Q includes unaudited financial statements and provides a continuing view of the company's financial position during the year. The report must be filed for each of the first three fiscal quarters of the company's fiscal year.

8K
Form 8K is the "current report" companies must file with the SEC to announce major events that

---

[11] http://www.sec.gov/answers/form10k.htm

[12] http://www.sec.gov/answers/form10k.htm

shareholders should know about.[13] Some events that require a company to file a Form 8K include bankruptcy, departure of directors or certain officers, and the creation of a direct financial obligation among others.

3. Proxy Solicitation
A proxy fight or battle can occur during a takeover. A proxy is a power of attorney to vote for the share ownership of another; to vote as a group. The acquiring corporation will persuade existing shareholders to vote out company management so that the company will be easier to takeover.

(a) Civil Liability

Section 14 of the Exchange Act

    a. Regulates the solicitation of proxies w/ respect to securities registered under Section 12

    b. Intended to promote the free exercise of the voting rights of SH by ensuring that proxies would be solicited w/ explanation to the SH of the real nature of the questions for which authority to cast votes is sought

    c. Rule 14a-9—prohibits solicitation of proxies which contain any materially false or misleading statement
      i. Implied private right of action exists
      ii. Standard of materiality is if there is a substantial likelihood that a reasonable shareholder would consider such information important in deciding how to vote
        1. Once materiality has been proved, there is sufficient causal

---

[13] http://www.sec.gov/answers/form8k.htm

relationship b/t the violation and the injury

2. Reliance not required
3. Loss causation not required
4. No deceptive or manipulative conduct need be shown
5. Plaintiff carries burden of demonstrating something false or misleading in what the statement expressly or impliedly declares about its subject
6. Nondisclosure of true purpose is not actionable. <u>As distinguished from</u> when there is material misstatement of reason, opinion, or belief as well as the factual basis therefore; then actionable

   iii. Applies where alleged disclosure deficiency contained in proxy information is material to shareholder assessment of management integrity, competence, and good faith.

4. Takeover Bids and Tender Offers

Takeover Bids
In a hostile takeover, one firm buys stock from another firm's shareholders directly behind management's back. The acquiring corporation pays a premium because it believes the target badly managed and thinks stock value will be raised with new management in place. The acquiring corporation is often operating against the target management that it wants to replace. The acquiring corporation identifies bad management; if can acquire stock and liquidate for profit the parts worth more than whole. The valuable going concern should be worth more than parts.

Shows no goodwill; no expectation of profits

a. Greenmail - potential acquirer buys shares, but target corporation buys back shares purchased by acquirer at a premium over market price to avoid takeover

Buying off one person provides no protection against later pursuers but corporation assets are depleted because of buyback and therefore the corporation is less attractive.

b. To avoid a hostile takeover, there is statutory power for directors to agree to purchase back shares of its own stock. There is a conflict of interest because the purchase may be to prevent a takeover and thus perpetuate the directors or officers in office.

EXCEPTIONS:

Interested / Inside Directors (those with personal and/or pecuniary interest): burden of proof on board of directors to prove stock repurchase was not acted upon primarily because of desire to keep themselves in office. The board of directors cannot act solely to entrench themselves.
- Must have proper business purpose before taking defensive measures
- Must prove acting in the best interests of shareholders

      ii.   Outside directors: burden of proof on the plaintiff to prove purchase was self-dealing or self-interest

- Burden of proof of board of directors met by showing of good faith and reasonable investigation; protected by the business judgment rule
- The business judgment rule protects the board of directors from allegations that it used improper judgments regarding business decisions. Unless the board of directors has blatantly violated some major rule of conduct, courts will not review or question its decisions or dealings.

Sufficient to show that takeover threatened corporate policy and effectiveness or "culture"

2. Defensive Measures During Hostile Takeover
   a. Defensive actions cannot be draconian (coercive or preclusive). The defensive action(s) must be reasonable in relation to the threat posed
   b. In the acquisition of its shares, a DE corporation may deal selectively w/its

stockholders, provided the directors have not acted out of a sole or primary purpose to entrench themselves in office.

c. Directors must show that they have reasonable grounds for believing that a danger to corporate policy and effectiveness existed because of another person's stock ownership (danger to corp. policy and effectiveness. Directors must act in good faith, make a reasonable investigation, and the response must be reasonable to the threat posed (proportionate).

d. Factors in opposing a takeover bid include:
   - inadequacy of price offered
   - nature and timing of offer
   - questions of illegality
   - impact on constituencies other than shareholders (creditors, employees)
   - risk of non-consummation
   - quality of securities being offered in exchange

A defense to a hostile takeover is reasonable **if** it is not coercive or preclusive.

   i. Coercive - aimed at forcing upon stockholders a management sponsored alternative to hostile over

   ii. Preclusive - if it deprives stockholders the right to receive all tender offers OR precludes bidder from seeking control by fundamentally restricting proxy contests or otherwise draconian (*Omnicare*)

e. Williams Act:
  i. The Williams Act, passed in 1968, is a series of amendments to the Exchange Act regarding cash tender offers
  ii. Requires full disclosure by bidder of its plans, background, and financing[14]
  iii. Purchaser of shares of publicly held corp. must identify itself and make similar disclosures within 10 days of purchase after acquiring 5% or more of any class of voting shares (promotes auctions and notifies incumbent mgmt.)
  iv. Mandates that highest price paid to any shareholder must be paid to all

f. Poison Pills
  A poison pill is strategy used by corporations to discourage a hostile takeover by another company. The target company attempts to make its stock less attractive to the acquirer. Two types exist:
  i. Flip-in—entitles the holder of each right except the acquirer and its affiliates to buy two shares of the target issuers common stock or other securities at half price.

---

[14] http://law.jrank.org/pages/11330/Williams-Act.html

Triggered by the actual acquisition of some percentage of the issuer's common stock.

- Results in value of stock received when right is exercised equal to two times the exercise price of the right
- Increases number of shares acquirer needs to purchase to gain control and makes more expensive to acquire

ii. Flip-over—feature triggered if acquisition of specified percentage of target's common stock and target subsequently merged into the acquirer or an affiliate; entitles each holder a right to purchase the common stock of the acquiring company at a discounted price.

- Results in dilution of acquiring companies shares; impairs capital structure
- Prevents two-tiered tender offers

iii. NOTE: poison pills are almost never actually exercised; they are leverage for the board of directors to promote an acquirer to negotiate with the board of directors. Often, the board will redeem poison pill in exchange for a higher price

iv. Impermissible poison pills:

- Dead hand—completely prevents board of directors installed by acquiring corporation from redeeming the pill; only board of directors who were there when the pill was "triggered" can redeem the pill (considered draconian)
- No-Hand—newly elected directors of target, whose majority nominated/supported by hostile bidder appointed by acquiring co. have to wait certain time period before redeeming pill

IMPERMISSIBLE: cannot deprive some or certain directors the ability to exercise powers of board of directors – must have the same rights as the predecessor board of directors

v. Poison Pill Defenses
- Anti-dilution provision - allows acquiring corporation to issue same amount of stock to current

stockholders so all shareholders keep same proportionate share and there is no dilution
- Call—right to purchase shares that it issues in merger at below market price (flip-over pill defense)

g. *Revlon* Duty - When sale of company becomes inevitable, board has duty to maximize the sale price. The board of directors becomes auctioneers. Must try to get highest price possible for shareholders.
   i. Cannot use further defense mechanisms and sole duty of board of directors is to obtain best price for shareholders
   ii. Cannot favor one purchaser over another
   iii. Must abandon long-term strategy and seek alternative sale or break-up by friendly bidders
   iv. Duty not triggered if preservation of long-term strategy favors one bidder over another even the terms of favored bidder are not as good in the short-term for shareholders
      - Board of directors must have bona fide good faith belief that favored bidder is better long-term approach; must be

reasonable in that belief

- If it is only a defensive strategy and the long term strategy is not abandoned, than *Unocal* duties are imposed.
- The adoption of structural safety devices (no shop clause, lock up contract) alone do not trigger *Revlon*.

v. Change in Control—results in diminution of voting power for those now in minority; where fundamental changes can be implemented by approval of majority including elections, amendments, mergers, asset sales, dissolution, etc.
- When change in control, board of directors given protection of business judgment rule as long as
  1. Board of directors used reasonable care in assessing threat of takeover before defending action
  2. Board of directors

                           adequately informs itself of all opportunities

          3. Responses to takeover threats are not draconian

          4. Does not put board of directors preferences above shareholders

          5. Seeks to protect shareholders over creditors, employees, community, etc.

h. Draconian—no shop provisions preventing other bidders, excessive termination fees to preferred bidder, unreasonable stock option provisions, lock-up provisions w/ no fiduciary out

i. Defensive measures adopted in good faith, after reasonable investigation if meets two step review

      i. Assess nature of threat and inadequacy of price offered; includes the nature and timing of offer, illegality, impact on creditors, customers; looks at short-term and long-term affect on shareholders

      ii. Reasonableness of defense tactics in light of threat; must look at in proportion to threat perceived; reasonableness

enhanced if majority of board
of directors outside and
independent

3. Friendly Takeover - acquires firm by negotiating
with managers and the merger is ratified by
shareholders
   a. Board of directors agree because of
   severance packages and consulting
   contract (golden parachute)
   b. A golden parachute decreases the
   amount of money that shareholders will
   be able to get from the
   merger/takeover, but shareholders still
   end up getting more than if no takeover
   existed

4. Shareholders impact:
   Decreases immediate value
   shareholders receive in transaction, but
   if mangers kill deal and deprive
   shareholders of any benefit then
   shareholders are stuck with bad
   management

5. Terms and Other
   a. Zone of Insolvency: "enterprise"
   director continues to owe duty to corp
   & expanded to included creditors; best
   interest of corp AND benefits of
   creditors over shareholders
   b. Stalking horse bidder: place first bid;
   often receive termination fee if bid not
   successful to compensate for starting
   bidding process

Tender Offers
A tender offer is a publicized bid to purchase shares of stock
at a premium over market price made directly to the target
corporation's shareholders with certain conditions

attached, frequently including a time limit for the duration of the offer, financing contingencies, a quantity limit on the number of shares that the bidder is willing to acquire.

Is there a tender offer? Apply an eight-factor test: *(SEC v. Carter Hawley)*

1. Active and widespread solicitation of public SH for the shares of issuer
2. Solicitation made for a substantial percentage of the issuer's stock
3. Offer to purchase made at a premium over the prevailing market price
4. Terms of the offer are firm rather than negotiable
5. Offer contingent on the tender of a fixed number of shares, often subject to a fixed maximum number to be purchased (the main factor)
6. Offer open only for a limited period of time
7. Offeree subjected to pressure to sell stock
8. Public announcements of a purchasing program concerning the target company precede or accompany rapid accumulation of large amounts of the target company's securities

d. **Section 13(d)(1)**—requires disclosure within ten days from any person who becomes the direct, indirect, or beneficial owner of 5% of a corporation's outstanding stock
   i. Must file a Schedule 13D which applies whether acquirer of 5% or more intends tender offer or not
   ii. Disclosure must include the background and identity of the offeror, source and amount of funds used, purpose of the contemplated purchases, number of shares owned, information regarding any special arrangements

involving the offer, and any additional information as the SEC may prescribe

iii. There is an implied private right of action for injunctive relief

iv. Loophole—because disclosure need not be made until 10 days after attaining 5% ownership, additional purchases may be made during this time period so long as it doesn't constitute a tender offer

> Allows potential acquirers to enhance ownership levels

v. SEC Tender Offer Rules

> **Rule 14d-9**: Requires subject corporation to file with the SEC a Schedule 14D-9 which calls for the disclosure of specified information including whether management recommends to shareholders to accept or reject offer. Additionally, the board of directors must disclose any conflicts of interest.
>
> > a. Rule 14d-10 - If a stock transaction is an integral part of a tender offer, and the consideration paid for the stock is different than that in the tender offer, then the transaction violates Rule 14d-10

(a) Federal & State Regulation of Takeovers[15]

The interplay between state and federal takeover regulation: the ways in which the federal/state interplay could led to some unintended (and usually undesirable) consequences.

---

[15] By Lisa Fairfax

Example 1: the way in which federal rules narrowed a bidder's prospective choices for acquiring a target's assets. At first glance, there appears to be three choices for structuring such an acquisition--an asset purchase, a merger, and a stock purchase, i.e., the tender offer for a public company. And yet, for many companies, federal rules often narrowed these choices down to one. On the one hand, tax laws made the asset deal unattractive. And on the other hand, federal court's interpretation of the Best Price Rule (the SEC rule requiring that the amount paid to any stockholder be the highest price paid to any other stockholder) made the stock deal less attractive. This is because federal courts had interpreted that Rule to apply to executive compensation paid in connection with a tender offer under the notion that such compensation was being paid as part of the consideration in a tender offer. Of course the SEC has now altered the Rule to make clear that it does not apply to executive compensation. When the question was raised regarding why it took the SEC so long to make such a clarification, it was observed that the SEC never intended the Rule to cover compensation arrangements, and thus did not think courts would interpret the rule in favor of such coverage. When it was clear that courts were "getting it wrong," the SEC realized the need to step in.

Example 2: the impact of federal rules on the state requirement for annual meetings. Indeed, federal proxy rules prohibit any proxy solicitation unless it is accompanied or preceded by an annual report including recent financial statements. This means that federal law would prohibit a company that does not have current financial information from soliciting the proxies it would need for its annual meeting, making it difficult for companies to comply with the state law requirement of holding an annual meeting. Several panelists noted that not only did the federal rule have unintended and undesirable consequences under state law, but it also had the peculiar impact of burdening a right that many corporations would rather not even exercise. To paraphrase Vice Chancellor Strine - it is a bit like telling your children that if they do not finish their homework, they will not have to eat their spinach. In other words, given some companies reluctance to hold annual meetings (particularly when there is the potential for stockholder confrontation) the federal rule may give such companies an easy out. And the companies most likely to get such an out are those companies experiencing some financial difficulties (hence the late filing), and thus the companies most likely to be confronted with shareholder discontent at the annual meeting. Again, this phenomenon represents another example of the federal and state rules working at cross purposes. Like the tender offer rules, the SEC recently amended its proxy solicitation rules to allow for exemptive relief from the provision regarding the type of information necessary for soliciting proxies. Hence, the SEC has reacted.

5. Liability for "Short-Swing" Profits

    <u>Defined</u>: Short-Swing Profits (§16(b))

    1. A company insider (officers, directors, and 10% owners) must pay to the corporation any profits they make within a 6-month period from buying and selling the corporation's stock.

        a. May be applied to any "matching" purchase and sale, or sale and purchase
        b. Whatever matching of purchase and sale transactions that produce the maximum profit are used
        c. An officer is an issuer's president, principal financial officer, principal acct.

officer, any VP in charge of a business unit, or others who make policy making decisions.

d. Only applies companies that register their stock under the 1934 Act.

e. To determine percentages, courts consider classes of stock separately. The shareholder will be liable for the short swing profits that he or she makes on any class of stock.

f. §16(b) covers convertible debt.

g. 10% ownership requirement strictly followed; may sell stock to bring ownership level below 10% then sell remaining shares; seller will only be liable to company for profits for those transactions while 10% owner (two-step sales permissible) Sales by former 10% not covered.

h. In a purchase-sale sequence, a beneficial owner must account for profits only if he is a beneficial owner before purchase. The rationale is that 10% owners are privy to inside information

i. Different classes of stock considered separately

V. S.E.C. RULE 10B-5: THE PROHIBITION OF FRAUD AND DECEIT

1. Market Manipulation

Rule 10b and Rule 10b-5 are the most common rules used to combat insider trading. The sale of stock by company insiders is legal insider trading. Illegal insider trading refers generally to buying or selling of securities, in breach of a fiduciary duty or other relationship of trust and confidence, while in possession of material, nonpublic information about the security. Insider trading violations may also include "tipping" such information, securities trading by the person "tipped," and securities trading by those who misappropriate such information.[16] Insider trading is legal once the material information has been made public, at which time the insider has no direct advantage over other investors.

2. The Jurisprudence of SEC Rule 10b-5

Rule 10(b) and Rule 10b-5 bar fraud and deception in the purchase or sale of securities whether done face to face, through a national securities exchange or in over-the-counter markets

The elements of a manipulation claim under Section 10(b) are: (1) fraudulent conduct; (2) in connection with the purchase or sale of securities; (3) through the means or instruments of transportation or communication in interstate commerce or the mails; and (4) with the requisite scienter (knowledge).

(a) Elements of 1934 Act Rule 10b-5

To state a market manipulation claim under Rule 10b-5(a) or (c), plaintiffs must allege: (1) that they were injured; (2) in connection with the purchase or sale of securities; (3) by relying on a market for securities; (4) controlled or artificially affected by the defendant's deceptive and manipulative conduct; and (5) that the defendant engaged in the manipulative conduct with knowledge of the falsity.[17]

---

[16] http://www.sec.gov/answers/insider.htm

[17] 17 CFR 240.10b-5

(b) Civil Liability for Violations

Although not explicit in Rule 10b or 10b-5, a private right of action exits for a violation, confirmed by the Supreme Court.[18] Both Rule 10(b) and Rule 10b-5 are very broad and include manipulative short selling and material misstatements and omissions.

3. Insider Trading

(a) Elements of the Violation

See above.

(b) Civil Liability

See above.

4. Corporate Misstatements

(a) Elements of the Violation

The plaintiff must show that misstatement or omission of fact is material. To be material, a reasonable investor would consider such information important in making an investment decision. The potential plaintiff need not show that the alleged incorrect information would have changed his investment decision.

1. Must be substantial likelihood that the disclosure of the omitted fact would have been viewed by the reasonable investor as having significantly altered the total mix of information made available

i. The plaintiff must establish that the defendant acted with scienter,

---

[18] *Superintendent of Ins. v. Bankers Life & Cas. Co.*, 404 U.S. 6, 13 n.9 (1971).

signifying knowing or intentional misconduct. Reckless, in most courts, may be sufficient to establish liability. Conduct must be "highly unreasonable" and represent an "extreme departure from the standards of ordinary care" for liability. Additionally, negligence is never sufficient

ii. The plaintiff must show he relied on the alleged misrepresentation and exercised due diligence

2. Provides a causal connection between defendant's wrongdoing and plaintiff's loss

3. Where failure to disclose, plaintiff's reliance is presumed

4. Fraud on the Market Theory (FMT)

    i. Presumption of reliance because theory postulates that investors assume that market price of a security is determined by available information and that no unsuspected fraudulent conduct has affected price

    ii. If positive proof of individual reliance were required, it would bar class actions

5. FMT is rebuttable presumption

    Must be shown that any material information which defendant's misstated or failed to disclose must have been transmitted to the public with a degree of intensity and credibility sufficient to effectively counterbalance misleading impression created by the defendant

6. Must determine whether the plaintiff performed due diligence to determine if reliance was justifiable. The plaintiff must prove that he/she did not act recklessly when engaging in transaction; factors looked at include:
    i. Sophistication and expertise of the plaintiff in financial and security matters
    ii. Existence of long standing business or personal relationship
    iii. Access to the relevant info
    iv. Existence of a fiduciary relationship
    v. Concealment of fraud
    vi. Opportunity to detect fraud
    vii. Whether plaintiff initiated stock transaction or sought to expedite transaction
    viii. Generality or specificity of misrepresentations
7. Bespeaks Caution Doctrine—where an offering statement contains future forecasts with adequate cautionary language, those statement are not actionable as securities fraud

    Establish causation between the defendant's wrongful conduct and plaintiff's loss

8. Loss Causation—but for misrepresentation, stock would not have declined in value
9. Transactional Causation—but for misrepresentation, plaintiff would not have purchased or sold security

Prove that manipulative or deceptive device was in connection with the purchase or sale of a security

10. Conduct must touch upon and be integral to the purchase or sale of the security
    i. Establish that the alleged primary violator had a duty to disclose
    ii. Prove the extent of damages suffered

11. Measure of damages is out-of-pocket loss

    Plaintiff must bring action within 2 yrs after violation was discovered by plaintiff or in no event greater than 5 yrs after violation

(b) Civil Liability[19]

Primary Liability for Secondary Actors
1. Civil liability for banks, issuers, broker-dealers and other "secondary" actors.
   - Primary liability under the evolving theory of "scheme" liability.
2. Liability under SEC enforcement provisions
   - Primary liability under securities laws
   - Secondary liability under traditional theories of aiding and abetting and "causing" primary violations.
   - Liability under the USA Patriot Act

---

[19] This section excerpted from Primary Liability for Secondary Actors by David H. Kistenbroker

3. Civil liability under § 10b for financial institutions and other secondary actors
    - Traditional Rule 10b-5 claim requires a material misstatement or omission
    - "Speaker" faces primary liability for a primary violation
4. Historically, financial institutions faced only secondary liability
    - aiding and abetting the fraudulent statements of others
    - Primary Liability for Secondary Actors
5. *Central Bank of Denver* (1994)
    - No private action for aiding and abetting
    - A financial institution may still face potential liability as a "primary violator"

Primary liability vs. non-actionable secondary actions

1. Courts have utilized three tests
    - "Bright Line" test – secondary actor must directly or indirectly make fraudulent statement: *Wright v. Ernst & Young, LLP* (2d Cir. 1998)
    - "Substantial Participation" test – significant role in preparing fraudulent statements: *In re Software Toolworks, Inc. Sec. Litig.* (9th Cir. 1994)
    - "Creation of Misrepresentation" test

2. "Creation of Misrepresentation" test:
    - First advocated by SEC in 1998 in amicus brief in *Klein v. Boyd* (3d Cir. 1998)

- Focus is on secondary actors' conduct rather than actual misstatements
- Relies on 10(b)-5(a) and (c) – i.e., device, scheme or artifice to defraud"
- First adopted in *In Re Enron Corp.* (2002)
  i. Lawyers drafted/approved false SEC filings
  ii. intimate involvement with transactions supported allegation they "created" the misstatements

3. "Scheme" liability and the courts

4. Appellate courts reject "scheme" liability:
   - 8th Circuit – *In re Charter Communications, Inc.*
   - 9th Circuit – *In re Homestore.com, Inc.*
     i. Third party vendors/arm's length transactions – no other role
     ii. Primary defendants failed to properly account for transactions
     iii. No misstatements, "deceptive" device or "manipulative" conduct

Developments in Secondary Actor Liability

1. District courts mixed on "scheme" liability
   - *In re Dynegy* (S.D. Texas 2004) - claim rejected
     i. Bank set up, executed two loans disguised as investment and cash flow

      ii.   No role in accounting/reporting transactions

      iii.   No allegations deceptive acts "coincided with sales of Dynegy securities."

- *Quaak v. Dexia, S.A.* (D.Mass 2005) – claim survives
  - i.   Bank financed "sham" entities used to record fictitious revenue
  - ii.   "Substantial participation" -- bank a 'primary architect' of the scheme.
  - iii.   Plaintiff subsequently filed amended complaint alleging direct liability; First Circuit vacated leave to appeal

2. District courts mixed on "scheme" liability
   - *In re Parmalat* (SDNY 2005) – mixed outcome
     - i.   Sham versus legitimate transactions
       - I.   The securitization and factoring of duplicate invoices for same goods was "deceptive device"
       - II.   Loans disguised as investments; deception resulted from company's description, therefore Citigroup/BoA's conduct not actionable
       - III.   No showing of reliance required in actionable transaction – no direct reliance is needed

3. District courts mixed on "scheme" liability
   - *In re Mutual Fund Investment Litig.* (D. Md. 2005) – mixed outcome
     i. Broker-dealers facilitated market-timed transactions
     ii. No liability for knowingly financing or clearing late trading
     iii. Liability for providing after-hours trading system, disabling time-stamp function

4. Line between primary and secondary liability remains undefined
   - Legitimacy of underlying transaction
     i. Transaction has true business purpose
     ii. Fraud is in accounting/reporting
   - Direct or substantial participation in deceptive acts
     i. "substantial participation" in *Quaak*
     ii. "orchestrating" in *Mutual Fund Litig.*
   - SEC Liability for "aiding and abetting" remains

5. **31 C.F.R. 103.122 Implements § 326 of the USA PATRIOT Act**
   - Final rule took effect on June 9, 2003, although broker-dealers had until October 1, 2003, to implement
   - The rules seek to protect the U.S. financial system from money laundering and terrorist financing.

- - Parallel rules exist for banks under § 103.121 and futures commission merchants and introducing brokers under § 103.123.
6. Requires Customer Identification Program (CIP) that, at a minimum, includes:
    - Identity verification procedures
    - Recordkeeping
    - Comparison with government lists
    - Customer notice
    - Reliance on another financial institution

7. Developments in Secondary Actor Liability

8. On May 22, 2006, the SEC announced its first-ever enforcement action under the USA PATRIOT Act
    - Action was brought against Crowell, Weedon, a broker-dealer.
        i. From 10/03 to 4/04, Crowell opened approximately 2,900 accounts.
        ii. In verifying customer's identities, Crowell relied on its registered reps' attestations that they had personal knowledge of the customers opening the accounts
        iii. The practice not documented in the firm's written customer

iv. identification program (CIP).

iv. Rather, the CIP stated the firm would verify the identity of new customers using certain non-documentary and documentary procedures, such as public data base searches and reviewing government issued identification.

9. Violation

- By failing to accurately document its CIP, Crowell violated the record-keeping and record retention requirements under the rule.

- Crowell consented to the issuance of an order that it cease and desist from committing or causing any violations and any future violations of Section 17(a) of the Securities Exchange Act and Rule 17a-8 thereunder.

5. Corporate Mismanagement

Absent deceptive or manipulative practices, mere instances of corporate mismanagement where the shareholders were treated unfairly by the fiduciary are not within the Rule.

VI. REGULATION OF THE SECURITIES BUSINESS

1. Conduct Regulation of Broker-Dealers

Broker-dealers, like other securities market participants, must comply with the general "antifraud" provisions of the federal securities laws. Broker-dealers must also comply with many requirements that are designed to maintain high industry standards. We discuss some of these provisions below.

(a) Antifraud Provisions:
(Sections 9(a), 10(b), and 15(c)(1) and (2))

The "antifraud" provisions prohibit misstatements or misleading omissions of material facts, and fraudulent or manipulative acts and practices, in connection with the purchase or sale of securities.[2] While these provisions are very broad, the Commission has adopted rules, issued interpretations, and brought enforcement actions that define some of the activities we consider manipulative, deceptive, fraudulent, or otherwise unlawful.[3] Broker-dealers must conduct their activities so as to avoid these kinds of practices.

1. Duty of Fair Dealing

Broker-dealers owe their customers a duty of fair dealing. This fundamental duty derives from the Act's antifraud provisions mentioned above. Under the so-called "shingle" theory, by virtue of engaging in the brokerage profession (*e.g.*, hanging out the broker-dealer's business sign, or "shingle"), a broker-dealer represents to its customers that it will deal fairly with them, consistent with the standards of the profession. Based on this important representation, the SEC, through interpretive statements and enforcement actions, and the courts, through case law, have set forth over time certain duties for broker-dealers. These include the duties to execute orders promptly, disclose certain material information (*i.e.*, information the customer would consider important as an investor), charge prices reasonably related to the prevailing market, and fully disclose any conflict of interest.

SRO rules also reflect the importance of fair dealing. For example, NASD members must comply with NASD's Rules of Fair Practice. These rules generally require broker-dealers to observe high standards of commercial honor and just and equitable principles of trade in conducting their business. The exchanges and the MSRB have similar rules.

2. Duty of Best Execution

The duty of best execution, which also stems from the Act's antifraud provisions, requires a broker-dealer to seek to obtain the most favorable terms available under the circumstances for its customer orders. This applies whether the broker-dealer is acting as agent or as principal.

The SRO rules also include a duty of best execution. For example, NASD members must use "reasonable diligence" to determine the best market for a security and buy or sell the security in that market, so that the price to the customer is as favorable as possible under prevailing market conditions.

3. Customer Confirmation Rule (Rule 10b-10 and MSRB rule G-15)

A broker-dealer must provide its customers, at or before the completion of a transaction, with certain information, including:

- the date, time, identity, price, and number of shares involved;

- its capacity (agent or principal) and its compensation (for agency trades, compensation includes its commission and whether it receives payment for order flow; and for principal trades, mark-up disclosure may be required);

- the source and amount of any third party remuneration it has received or will receive;[5]

- other information, both general (such as, if the broker-dealer is not a SIPC member) and transaction-specific (such as the yield, in most transactions involving debt securities).

A broker-dealer may also be obligated under the antifraud provisions of the Act to disclose additional information to the customer at the time of his or her investment decision.

4. Disclosure of Credit Terms *(Rule 10b-16)*

Broker-dealers must notify customers purchasing securities on credit about the credit terms and the status of their accounts. A broker-dealer must establish procedures for disclosing this information before it extends credit to a customer for the purchase of securities. A broker-dealer must give the customer this information at the time the account is opened, and must also provide credit customers with account statements at least quarterly.

5. Restrictions on Short Sales *(Regulation SHO)*

A "short sale" is generally a sale of a security that the seller doesn't own. Exchange Act Rule 10a-1 is designed to limit short selling in a declining market. The rule generally bars a person from selling a covered security that he or she does not own, unless the sale is at a price above the price of the last sale, or at the last sale price if that price was above the next preceding different price.

Regulation SHO was adopted in 2004 to update short sale regulation in light of numerous market developments since short sale regulation was first adopted in 1938. Compliance with Regulation SHO began on January 3, 2005. Some of the goals of Regulation SHO include:

- Establishing uniform "locate" and "close-out" requirements in order to address problems associated with failures to deliver, including potentially abusive "naked" short selling.

  Locate Requirement: Regulation SHO requires a broker-dealer to have reasonable grounds to believe that the security can be borrowed so that it can be delivered on the date delivery is due before effecting a short sale order in any equity security. This "locate" must be made and documented prior to effecting the short sale. Market makers engaged in bona fide market making are exempted from the "locate" requirement.

  "Close-out" Requirement: Regulation SHO imposes additional delivery requirements on broker-dealers for securities in which there are a relatively substantial number of extended delivery failures at a registered clearing agency ("threshold securities"). For instance, with limited exception, Regulation SHO requires brokers and dealers that are participants of a registered clearing agency to take action to "close-out" failure-to-deliver positions ("open fails") in threshold securities that have persisted for 13 consecutive settlement days. Closing out requires the broker or dealer to purchase securities of like kind and quantity. Until the position is closed out, the broker or dealer and any broker or dealer for which it clears transactions (for

example, an introducing broker) may not effect further short sales in that threshold security without borrowing or entering into a bona fide agreement to borrow the security (known as the "pre-borrowing" requirement).

- Temporarily suspending Commission and SRO short sale price tests in a group of securities to evaluate the overall effectiveness and necessity of such restrictions. The Commission will study the impact of relaxing the price tests for a period of one year.

- Creating uniform order marking requirements for sales of all equity securities. This means that orders you place with your broker-dealer must be marked "long," "short," or "short exempt."

6. Trading During an Offering *(Regulation M)*

Regulation M is designed to protect the integrity of the securities trading market as an independent pricing mechanism by governing the activities of underwriters, issuers, selling security holders, and other participants in connection with a securities offering. These rules are aimed at preventing persons having an interest in an offering from influencing the market price for the offered security in order to facilitate a distribution.

Rule 101 of Regulation M generally prohibits underwriters, broker-dealers and other distribution participants from bidding for, purchasing, or attempting to induce any person to bid for or purchase, any security which is the subject of a distribution until the applicable restricted period has ended. An offering's "restricted period" begins either one or five business days (depending on the trading volume value of the offered security and the public float value of the issuer) before the day of the offering's pricing and ends upon completion of the distribution.

Rule 101 contains various exceptions that are designed to permit an orderly distribution of securities and limit disruption in the market for the securities being distributed. For example, underwriters can continue to trade in actively-traded securities of larger issuers (securities with an average daily trading volume, or ADTV, value of $1 million or more and whose issuers have a public float value of at least $150 million). In addition, the following activities, among others, may be excepted from Rule 101, if they meet specified conditions:

- disseminating research reports;

- making unsolicited purchases;

- purchasing a group, or "basket" of 20 or more securities;

- exercising options, warrants, rights, and convertible securities;

- effecting transactions that total less than 2% of the security's ADTV; and

- effecting transactions in securities sold to "qualified institutional buyers."

Rule 102 of Regulation M prohibits issuers, selling security holders, and their affiliated purchasers from bidding for, purchasing, or attempting to induce any person to bid for or purchase, any security which is the subject of a distribution until after the applicable restricted period.

Rule 103 of Regulation M governs passive market making by broker-dealers participating in an offering of a NASDAQ security.

Rule 104 of Regulation M governs stabilization transactions, syndicate short covering activity, and penalty bids.

Rule 105 of Regulation M prevents manipulative short sales in anticipation of an offering by prohibiting investors from the covering certain short sales with securities purchased in the offering.

7. Restrictions on Insider Trading

The SEC and the courts interpret Section 10(b) and Rule 10b-5 under the Act to bar the use by any person of material non-public information in the purchase or sale of securities, whenever that use violates a duty of trust and confidence owed to a third party. Section 15(f) of the Act specifically requires broker-dealers to have and enforce written policies and procedures reasonably designed to prevent their employees from misusing material non-public information. Because employees in the investment banking operations of broker-dealers frequently have access to material non-public information, firms need to create procedures designed to limit the flow of this information so that their employees cannot use the information in the trading of securities. Broker-dealers can use these information barriers as a defense to a claim of insider trading. Such procedures typically include:

- training to make employees aware of these restrictions;

- employee trading restrictions;

- physical barriers;

- isolation of certain departments; and

- limitations on investment bank proprietary trading.[6]

8. Restrictions on Private Securities Transactions

NASD Rule 3040 provides that "no person associated with a member shall participate in any manner in a private securities transaction" except in accordance with the provisions of the rule. To the extent that any such transactions are permitted under the rule, prior to participating in any private securities transaction, the associated person must provide written notice to the member firm as described in the rule. If compensation is involved, the member firm must approve or disapprove the proposed transaction, record it in its books and records, and supervise the transaction as if it were executed on behalf of the member firm. Other conditions may also apply. In addition, private securities transactions of an associated person may be subject to an analysis under Exchange Act Section 10(b) and Rule 10-5, as well as the broker-dealer supervisory provisions of Section 15(f) (described in Part V.A.7, above) and Section 15(b)(4)(E), and other relevant statutory or regulatory provisions.

(b) Analysts and Regulation AC

Regulation AC (or Regulation Analyst Certification) requires brokers, dealers, and persons associated with brokers or dealers that publish, distribute, or circulate research reports to include in those reports a certification that the views expressed in the report accurately reflect the analyst's personal views. The report must also disclose whether the analyst received compensation for the views expressed in the report. If the analyst has received related compensation, the broker, dealer, or associated person must disclose its amount, source, and purpose. Regulation AC applies to all brokers and dealers, as well as to those persons associated with a broker or dealer that fall within the definition of "covered person." Regulation AC also requires that broker-dealers keep records of analyst certifications relating to public appearances.

In addition to Commission rules, analyst conduct is governed by SRO rules, such as NASD Rule 2711 and NYSE Rule 472. The SRO rules impose restrictions on analyst compensation, personal trading activities, and involvement in investment banking activities. The SRO rules also include disclosure requirements for research reports and public appearances.

(c) **Trading by Members of Exchanges, Brokers and Dealers (Section 11(a))**

Broker-dealers that are members of national securities exchanges are subject to additional regulations regarding transactions they effect on exchanges. For example, except under certain conditions, they generally cannot effect transactions on exchanges for their own accounts, the accounts of their associated persons, or accounts that they or their associated persons manage. Exceptions from this general rule include transactions by market makers, transactions routed through other members, and transactions that yield to other orders. Exchange members may wish to seek guidance from their exchange regarding these provisions.

(d) **Extending Credit on New Issues; Disclosure of Capacity as Broker or Dealer** *(Section 11(d))*

Section 11(d)(1) of the Act generally prohibits a broker-dealer that participates in the distribution of a new issue of securities from extending credit to customers in connection with the new issue during the distribution period and for 30 days thereafter. Sales by a broker-dealer of mutual fund shares and variable insurance product units are deemed to constitute participation in the distribution of a new issue. Therefore, purchase of mutual fund shares or variable product units using credit extended or arranged by the broker-dealer during the distribution period is a violation of Section 11(d)(1). However, Exchange Act Rule 11d1-2 permits a broker-dealer to extend credit to a customer on newly sold mutual fund shares and variable insurance product units after the customer has owned the shares or units for 30 days.

Section 11(d)(2) of the Act requires a broker-dealer to disclose in writing, at or before the completion of each transaction with a customer, whether the broker-dealer is acting in the capacity of broker or dealer with regard to the transaction.

(e) **Order Execution Obligations** *(Rules 602-604 of Regulation NMS)*

Broker-dealers that are exchange specialists or Nasdaq market makers must comply with particular rules regarding publishing quotes and handling customer orders. These two types of broker-dealers have special functions in the securities markets, particularly because they trade for their own accounts while also handling orders for customers. These rules, which include the "Quote Rule" and the "Limit Order Display Rule," increase the information that is publicly available concerning the prices at which investors may buy and sell exchange-listed and Nasdaq National Market System securities.

The Quote Rule requires specialists and market makers to provide quotation information to their self-regulatory organization for dissemination to the public. The quote information that the specialist or market maker provides must reflect the best prices at which he is willing to trade (the lowest price the dealer will accept from a customer to sell the securities and the highest price the dealer will pay a customer to purchase the securities). A specialist or market maker may still trade at better prices in certain private trading systems, called electronic communications networks, or "ECNs," without publishing an improved quote. This is true only when the ECN itself publishes the improved prices and makes those prices available to the investing public. Thus, the Quote Rule ensures that the public has access to the best prices at which specialists and market makers are willing to trade even if those prices are in private trading systems.

Limit orders are orders to buy or sell securities at a specified price. The Limit Order Display Rule requires that specialists and market makers publicly display certain limit orders they receive from customers. If the limit order is for a price that is better than the specialist's or market maker's quote, the specialist or market maker must publicly display it. The rule benefits investors because the publication of trading interest at prices that improve specialists' and market makers' quotes present investors with improved pricing opportunities.

(f) Penny Stock Rules *(Rules 15g-2 through 15g-9, Schedule 15G)*

Most broker-dealers that effect transactions in "penny stocks" have certain enhanced suitability and disclosure obligations to their customers.[7] A penny stock is generally defined as any equity security other than a security that: (a) is an NMS stock[8] listed on a "grandfathered" national securities exchange, (b) is an NMS stock listed on a national securities exchange or an automated quotation system sponsored by a registered national securities association (including Nasdaq) that satisfies certain minimum quantitative listing standards, (c) has a transaction price of five dollars or more, (d) is issued by a registered investment company or by the Options Clearing Corporation, (e) is a listed security futures product, or (f) is a security whose issuer has met certain net tangible assets or average revenues.[9] Penny stocks include the equity securities of private companies with no active trading market if they do not qualify for one of the exclusions from the definition of penny stock.

Before a broker-dealer that does not qualify for an exemption[10] may effect a solicited transaction in a penny stock for or with the account of a customer it must: (1) provide the customer with a risk disclosure document, as set forth in Schedule 15G, and receive a signed and dated acknowledgement of receipt of that document from the customer[11]; (2) approve the customer's account for transactions in penny stocks, provide the customer with a suitability statement, and receive a signed a dated copy of that statement from the customer; and (3) receive the customer's written agreement to the transaction.[12] The broker-dealer also must wait at least two business days after sending the customer the risk disclosure document and the suitability statement before effecting the transaction. In addition, Exchange Act Rules 15g-3 through 15g-6 generally require a broker-dealer to give each penny stock customer:

- information on market quotations and, where appropriate, offer and bid prices;

- the aggregate amount of any compensation received by the broker-dealer in connection with such transaction;

- the aggregate amount of cash compensation that any associated person of the broker-dealer, who is a natural person and who has communicated with the customer concerning the transaction at or prior to the customer's transaction order, other than a person whose function is solely clerical or ministerial, has received or will receive from any source in connection with the transaction; and

- monthly account statements showing the market value of each penny stock held in the customer's account.

(g) Privacy of Consumer Financial Information (Regulation S-P)

Regulation S-P requires broker-dealers to provide their customers with initial, annual and revised privacy notices, which must be clear and conspicuous, and which must accurately reflect their policies and practices. The regulation also requires broker-dealers to adopt appropriate policies and procedures to protect customer records and information. In addition, it limits disclosures to non-affiliated third parties of account number information for use in telemarketing, direct mail marketing and e-mail marketing. Subject to certain exceptions, Regulation S-P also requires broker-dealers to allow consumers to opt out of disclosures of their nonpublic personal information to non-affiliates.

Broker-dealers, including foreign broker-dealers registered with the Commission and unregistered broker-dealers in the United States, must comply with Regulation S-P, even if their consumers are non-U.S. persons or if they conduct their activities through non-U.S. offices or branches.

(h) Regulation ATS: Electronic Broker-Dealer Trading Systems

Certain entities carry out some functions traditionally associated with exchanges by, for example, using an electronic platform to collect and execute orders in securities. Such an entity may be required to register with the Commission as an alternative trading system (ATS). An ATS is any organization, association, person, group of persons, or system that constitutes, maintains, or provides a marketplace or facilities for bringing together purchasers and sellers of securities or for otherwise performing with respect to securities the functions commonly performed by a stock exchange. An entity would not be considered an ATS if it sets rules governing the conduct of subscribers other than the conduct of such subscribers' conduct on the entity or if it disciplines subscribers other than by exclusion from trading. In such a case, the entity may be required to register as a national securities exchange or obtain a Commission exemption from exchange registration based on limited trading volume. An ATS that chooses to be subject to Regulation ATS must, among other things, register as a broker-dealer and file an initial operation report on Form ATS. The Commission does not approve an ATS; however, the ATS must file the initial operation report at least 20 days before commencing operation, and the Form ATS is not considered filed unless it complies with all applicable requirements. An ATS also must provide a quarterly report on Form ATS-R.

(i) Regulation NMS

Regulation NMS, adopted by the SEC in April 2005, contains four interrelated topics that are designed to modernize the regulatory structure of the U.S. equity markets. The substantive topics addressed by Regulation NMS are (1) order protection, (2) intermarket access, (3) sub-penny pricing, and (4) market data.

- The "Order Protection Rule" requires trading centers to establish, maintain, and enforce written policies and procedures reasonably designed to prevent the execution of trades at prices inferior to protected quotations displayed by other trading centers, subject to an applicable exception. To be protected, a quotation must be immediately and automatically accessible.

- The "Access Rule" requires fair and non-discriminatory access to quotations, establishes a limit on access fees to harmonize the pricing of quotations across different trading centers, and requires each national securities exchange and national securities association to adopt, maintain, and enforce written rules that prohibit their members from engaging in a pattern or practice of displaying quotations that lock or cross automated quotations.

- The "Sub-Penny Rule" prohibits market participants from accepting, ranking, or displaying orders, quotations, or indications of interest in a pricing increment smaller than a penny, except for orders, quotations, or indications of interest that are priced at less than $1.00 per share.

- The "Market Data Rules" update the requirements for consolidating, distributing, and displaying market information. In addition, amendments to the joint industry plans for disseminating market information modify the formulas for allocating plan revenues among the self-regulatory organizations and broaden participation in plan governance.

In addition, Regulation NMS updates and streamlines the existing Exchange Act rules governing the national market system previously adopted under Section 11A of the Exchange Act, and consolidates them into a single regulation.

Compliance with the Order Protection Rule and the Access Rule will begin with a small group of representative national market system stocks, to allow market participants to verify the functionality of their systems and procedures necessary to effectively comply with the rules. This first phase will begin on June 29, 2006 and end on August 30, 2006. On August 31, 2006, trading centers will be required to begin trading all national market system stocks pursuant to the requirements of Order Protection Rule and the Access Rule. The compliance date for the amendment to the formula that allocates revenues among the self-regulatory organizations will be September 1, 2006. The compliance date for all other portions of Regulation NMS will be August 29, 2005.

(j) Investment Adviser Registration

Broker-dealers offering certain types of accounts and services may also be subject to regulation under the Investment Advisers Act.[13] For example, a broker-dealer that offers fee-based accounts (*i.e.*, accounts that charge an asset-based or fixed fee rather than a commission, mark-up, or mark-down) must treat those accounts as advisory unless the broker-dealer provides investment advice that is solely incidental to its brokerage services and also makes certain disclosures about the nature of the account (*e.g.*, the account is a brokerage account, not an advisory account). Also, a broker-dealer must treat each account over which it exercises investment discretion as an advisory account, unless the investment discretion is granted by a customer on a temporary or limited basis.

Furthermore, a broker-dealer must treat an account as advisory if the broker-dealer charges a separate fee for, or separately contracts to provide, advisory services; or if the broker-dealer provides advice as part of a financial plan or in connection with financial planning services and: (i) holds itself out to the public as a financial planner or as providing financial planning services; (ii) delivers to its customer a financial plan; or (iii) represents to the customer that the advice is provided as part of a financial plan or financial planning services. Financial planning services typically involve assisting clients in identifying long-term economic goals, analyzing their current financial situation, and preparing a comprehensive financial program to achieve those goals. A financial plan generally seeks to address a wide spectrum of a client's long-term financial needs, including insurance, savings, tax and estate planning, and investments, taking into consideration the client's goals and situation, including anticipated retirement or other employee benefits. Typically, what distinguishes financial planning from other types of advisory services is the breadth and scope of the advisory services provided.

A broker-dealer that is registered under the Exchange Act and registered under the Advisers Act would be an investment adviser solely with respect to those accounts for which it provides services that subject the broker-dealer to the Advisers Act.

2. Financial Responsibility of Broker-Dealers

Broker-dealers must meet certain financial responsibility requirements, including:

- maintaining minimum amounts of liquid assets, or net capital;
- taking certain steps to safeguard the customer funds and securities; and
- making and preserving accurate books and records.

(a) Net Capital Rule *(Rule 15c3-1)*

The purpose of this rule is to require a broker-dealer to have at all times enough liquid assets to promptly satisfy the claims of customers if the broker-dealer goes out of business. Under this rule, broker-dealers must maintain minimum net capital levels based upon the type of securities activities they conduct and based on certain financial ratios. For example, broker-dealers that clear and carry customer accounts generally must maintain net capital equal to the greater of $250,000 or two percent of aggregate debit items. Broker-dealers that do not clear and carry customer accounts can operate with lower levels of net capital.

(b) Use of Customer Balances *(Rule 15c3-2)*

Broker-dealers that use customers' free credit balances in their business must establish procedures to provide specified information to those customers, including:

- the amount due to those customers;

- the fact that such funds are not segregated and may be used by the broker-dealer in its business; and

- the fact that such funds are payable on demand of the customer.

(c) **Customer Protection Rule (Rule 15c3-3)**

This rule protects customer funds and securities held by broker-dealers. Under the rule, a broker-dealer must have possession or control of all fully-paid or excess margin securities held for the account of customers, and determine daily that it is in compliance with this requirement. The broker-dealer must also make periodic computations to determine how much money it is holding that is either customer money or obtained from the use of customer securities. If this amount exceeds the amount that it is owed by customers or by other broker-dealers relating to customer transactions, the broker-dealer must deposit the excess into a special reserve bank account for the exclusive benefit of customers. This rule thus prevents a broker-dealer from using customer funds to finance its business.

(d) **Required Books, Records and Reports (Rules 17a-3, 17a-4, 17a-5, 17a-11)**

Broker-dealers must make and keep current books and records detailing, among other things, securities transactions, money balances, and securities positions. They also must keep records for required periods and furnish copies of those records to the SEC on request. These records include e-mail. Broker-dealers also must file with the SEC periodic reports, including quarterly and annual financial statements. The annual statements generally must be certified by an independent public accountant. In addition, broker-dealers must notify the SEC and the appropriate SRO[15] regarding net capital, recordkeeping, and other operational problems, and in some cases file reports regarding those problems, within certain time periods. This gives us and the SROs early warning of these problems.

(e) Risk Assessment Req. (Rules 17h-1T and 17h-2T)

Certain broker-dealers must maintain and preserve certain information regarding those affiliates, subsidiaries and holding companies whose business activities are reasonably likely to have a material impact on their own financial and operating condition (including the broker-dealer's net capital, liquidity, or ability to conduct or finance operations). Broker-dealers must also file a quarterly summary of this information. This information is designed to permit the SEC to assess the impact these entities may have on the broker-dealer.

3. Other Requirements

In addition to the provisions discussed above, broker-dealers must comply with other requirements. These include:

- submitting to Commission and SRO examinations;

- participating in the lost and stolen securities program;

- complying with the fingerprinting requirement;

- maintaining and reporting information regarding their affiliates;

- following certain guidelines when using electronic media to deliver information; and

- maintaining an anti-money laundering program.

(a) Examinations and Inspections (Rules 15b2-2 and 17d-1)

Broker-dealers are subject to examination by the SEC and the SROs. The appropriate SRO generally inspects newly-registered broker-dealers for compliance with applicable financial responsibility rules within six months of registration, and for compliance with all other regulatory requirements within twelve months of registration. A broker-dealer must permit the SEC to inspect its books and records at any reasonable time.

(b) Lost and Stolen Securities Program (Rule 17f-1)

In general, all broker-dealers must register in the lost and stolen securities program. The limited exceptions include broker-dealers that effect securities transactions exclusively on the floor of a national securities exchange solely for other exchange members and do not receive or hold customer securities, and broker-dealers whose business does not involve handling securities certificates. Broker-dealers must report losses, thefts, and instances of counterfeiting of securities certificates on Form X-17F-1A, and, in some cases, must make inquiries regarding securities certificates coming into their possession. Broker-dealers file these reports and inquiries with the Securities Information Center (SIC), which operates the program for the SEC.

(c) Fingerprinting Requirement (Rule 17f-2)

Generally, every partner, officer, director, or employee of a broker-dealer must be fingerprinted and submit his or her fingerprints to the U.S. Attorney General. This requirement does not apply, however, to broker-dealers that sell only certain securities that are not ordinarily evidenced by certificates (such as mutual funds and variable annuities) or to persons who do not sell securities, have access to securities, money or original books and records, and do not supervise persons engaged in such activities. A broker-dealer claiming an exemption must comply with the notice requirements of Rule 17f-2. SRO members may obtain fingerprint cards from their SRO and should submit completed fingerprint cards to the SRO for forwarding to the Attorney General.

(d) Use of Electronic Media by Broker-Dealers

The Commission has issued two interpretive releases discussing the issues that broker-dealers should consider in using electronic media for delivering information to customers. These issues include the following:

- Will the customer have notice of and access to the communication?

- Will there be evidence of delivery?

- Did the broker-dealer take reasonable precautions to ensure the integrity, confidentiality, and security of any personal financial information?

(e) Electronic Signatures (E-SIGN)

Broker-dealers should also consider the impact, if any, that the Electronic Signatures in Global and National Commerce Act (commonly known as E-SIGN), Pub. L. No. 106-229, 114 Stat. 464 (2000) [15 U.S.C. §7001], has on their ability to deliver information to customers electronically.

(f) Anti-Money Laundering Program

Broker-dealers have broad obligations under the Bank Secrecy Act ("BSA") to guard against money laundering and terrorist financing through their firms. The BSA, its implementing regulations, and Rule 17a-8 under the Exchange Act require broker-dealers to file reports or retain records relating to suspicious transactions, customer identity, large cash transactions, cross-border currency movement, foreign bank accounts and wire transfers, among other things.

The BSA, as amended by the USA PATRIOT Act, as well as SRO rules (*e.g.*, NASD Rule 3011 and NYSE Rule 445), also requires all broker-dealers to have anti-money laundering compliance programs in place. Firms must develop and implement a written anti-money laundering compliance program, approved in writing by a member of senior management, which is reasonably designed to achieve and monitor the member's ongoing compliance with the requirements of the Bank Secrecy Act and its implementing regulations. Under this obligation, firms must:

- establish and implement policies and procedures that can be reasonably expected to detect and cause the reporting of suspicious transactions;

- establish and implement policies, procedures, and internal controls reasonably designed to achieve compliance with the BSA and implementing regulations;

- provide for independent testing for compliance, to be conducted by member personnel or by a qualified outside party;

- designate and identify to the SROs an individual or individuals responsible for implementing and monitoring the day-to-day operations and internal controls of the program and provide prompt notification regarding any change in such designation(s); and

- provide ongoing training for appropriate personnel.

VII.   INVESTMENT COMPANY ACT OF 1940: THE REGULATION OF INVESTMENT COMPANIES

1.   Coverage of the 1940 Act

The Investment Company Act of 1940 defines the responsibilities and limitations placed on fund companies that offer investment products to the public. A fund company invests the pooled assets of investors in securities. The focus of the Act is on disclosure to the investing public of information about the fund and its investment objectives, as well as on investment company structure and operations.[20]

(a) Types of Investment Companies

Under Section 4 for the Act, investment companies are divided into three principal classes. They are: 1) Face-amount certificate company; 2) unit investment trust; 3) management company.

A face certificate company is an investment company which is engaged or proposes to engage in the business of issuing face-amount certificates of the installment type, or which has been engaged in such business and has any such certificate outstanding.

A unit investment trust is an investment company which (A) is organized under a trust indenture, contract of custodianship or agency, or similar instrument, (B) does not have a board of directors, and (C) issues only redeemable securities, each of which represents an undivided interest in a unit of

---

[20] http://www.sec.gov/about/laws.shtml

specified securities; but does not include a voting trust.

A management company means any investment company other than a face-amount certificate company or a unit investment trust.[21]

(b) Exemptions

Section 6 of the Act lists a number of exemptions including corporations reorganized by a court if A) such company was not an investment company at the commencement of such reorganization proceedings, (B) at the conclusion of such proceedings all outstanding securities of such company were owned by creditors of such company or by persons to whom such securities were issued on account of creditors' claims, and (C) more than 50% of the voting securities of such company, and securities representing more than 50% of the net asset value of such company, are currently owned beneficially by not more than twenty-five persons; but such exemption shall terminate if any security of which such company is the issuer is offered for sale or sold to the public after the conclusion of such proceedings by the issuer or by or through any underwriter.[22]

Additionally, closed-end investment companies, if the securities is proposals to sell do not exceed $10 million, are exempt form the Investment Company Act of 1940. Furthermore, no security of which such company is the issuer has been or is proposed to be sold, in connection with a public offering, to any person who is not a resident of the State under the laws of which such company is organized or otherwise created.

---

[21] http://www.law.uc.edu/CCL/InvCoAct/sec4.html

[22] http://www.law.uc.edu/CCL/InvCoAct/sec6.html

2. Regulation of Fund Activities

Registered investment companies are not allowed to 1) purchase securities on margin, except if necessary for short to credit to facilitate the clearance of transactions; 2) short-sell securities; or to participate on a joint or a joint and several basis in any trading account in securities, except in connection with an underwriting in which such registered company is a participant.[23]

According to Section 12 of the Investment Company Act of 1940, any investment company that wishes to distribute securities of its own must use an underwriter. It shall be unlawful for any registered diversified company to make any commitment as underwriter, if immediately thereafter the amount of its outstanding underwriting commitments, plus the value of its investments in securities of issuers (other than investment companies) of which it owns more than 10 per centum of the outstanding voting securities, exceeds 25 percent of the value of its total assets.

Section 2(a)(11) of the Securities Act defines underwriter as any person who has purchased from an issuer (i) with a view to, or (ii) offers or sells for an issuer in connection with, the distribution of any security, or (iii) participates or has a direct or indirect participating in any such undertaking

Limitations on Acquisition by Investment Companies of Securities of other Specific Businesses

A registered investment company may not purchase or acquire any security issued by any other investment company, and for any investment company purchase or otherwise acquire any security issued by any registered investment company, if the acquiring company and any

---

[23] http://www.law.uc.edu/CCL/InvCoAct/sec12.html

company or companies controlled by it immediately after such purchase or acquisition own in the aggregate:

i.   more than 3% of the total outstanding voting stock of the acquired company;

ii.   securities issued by the acquired company having an aggregate value in excess of 5% of the value of the total assets of the acquiring company; or

iii.   securities issued by the acquired company and all other investment companies (other than treasury stock of the acquiring company) having an aggregate value in excess of 10% of the value of the total assets of the acquiring company.

3.   Management and Control

(a) Shareholders, Directors and Offers

Shareholders

A registered management investment company, other than a small business investment company registered on Form N-5, is required to file annual and quarterly reports pursuant to section 13(a) or 15(d) of the Securities Exchange Act of 1934.[24]

Offers

Approval is needed by the SEC for exchanges of securities on basis other than relative net asset value. It shall be unlawful for any registered open-end company or any principal underwriter for such a company to make or cause to be made an offer to the holder of a security of such company or of any other open-end investment company to exchange his security for a security in the same or another

---

[24] 17 CFR 270.30d-1

such company on any basis other than the relative net asset values of the respective securities to be exchanged, unless the terms of the offer have first been submitted to and approved by the SEC or are in accordance with such rules and regulations as the SEC may have prescribed. For the purposes of this section, (A) an offer by a principal underwriter means an offer communicated to holders of securities of a class or series but does not include an offer made by such principal underwriter to an individual investor in the course of a retail business conducted by such principal underwriter, and (B) the net asset value means the net asset value which is in effect for the purpose of determining the price at which the securities, or class or series of securities involved, are offered for sale to the public either (1) at the time of the receipt by the offeror of the acceptance of the offer or (2) at such later times as is specified in the offer.[25]

Directors:

Directors of investment companies must be elected to that office by the holders of the outstanding voting securities of such company, at an annual or a special meeting duly called for that purpose. If vacancies exist between such meetings, they may be filled in any otherwise legal manner if immediately after filling any such vacancy at least two-thirds of the directors then holding office shall have been elected to such office by the holders of the outstanding voting securities of the company at such an annual or special meeting.

Any vacancy on the board of directors of a registered investment company which must be filled by a person who is not an interested person of either party to a transaction shall be filled only by a

---

[25] 17 CFR 270.11a-3

person (1) who has been selected and proposed for election by a majority of the directors of such company who are not such interested persons, and (2) who has been elected by the holders of the outstanding voting securities of such company, except that in the case of the death, disqualification, or bona fide resignation of an elected director.[26]

(b) Management Compensation and Exemptions

Rule 205-3 – Exemption From the Compensation Prohibition of Section 205(a)(1) for Investment Advisers

(a) General. The provisions of section 205(a)(1) of the Act [15 U.S.C. 80b-5(a)(1)] will not be deemed to prohibit an investment adviser from entering into, performing, renewing or extending an investment advisory contract that provides for compensation to the investment adviser on the basis of a share of the capital gains upon, or the capital appreciation of, the funds, or any portion of the funds, of a client, Provided, That the client entering into the contract subject to this section is a qualified client, as defined in paragraph (d)(1) of this section.

(b) Identification of the client. In the case of a private investment company, as defined in paragraph (d)(3) of this section, an investment company registered under the Investment Company Act of 1940, or a business development company, as defined in section 202(a)(22) of the Act [15 U.S.C. 80b-2(a)(22)], each equity owner of any such company (except for the investment adviser entering into the contract and any other equity owners not charged a fee on the basis of a share of

---

[26] http://www.sec.gov/about/laws/ica40.pdf

90

capital gains or capital appreciation) will be considered a client for purposes of paragraph (a) of this section.

(c) Transition rule. An investment adviser that entered into a contract before August 20, 1998, and satisfied the conditions of this section as in effect on the date that the contract was entered into will be considered to satisfy the conditions of this section; Provided, however, that this section will apply with respect to any natural person or company who is not a party to the contract prior to and becomes a party to the contract after August 20, 1998.

(d) Definitions. For the purposes of this section:

(1) The term "qualified client" means:

(i) A natural person who or a company that immediately after entering into the contract has at least $750,000 under the management of the investment adviser;

(ii) A natural person who or a company that the investment adviser entering into the contract (and any person acting on his behalf) reasonably believes, immediately prior to entering into the contract, either:

(A) Has a net worth (together, in the case of a natural person, with assets held jointly with a spouse) of more than $1,500,000 at the time the contract is entered into; or

(B) Is a qualified purchaser as defined in section 2(a)(51)(A) of the Investment Company Act of 1940 [15 U.S.C. 80a-2(a)(51)(A)] at the time the contract is entered into; or

(iii) A natural person who immediately prior to entering into the contract is:

(A) An executive officer, director, trustee, general partner, or person serving in a similar capacity, of the investment adviser; or

(B) An employee of the investment adviser (other than an employee performing solely clerical, secretarial or administrative functions with regard to the investment adviser) who, in connection with his or her regular functions or duties, participates in the investment activities of such investment adviser, provided that such employee has been performing such functions and duties for or on behalf of the investment adviser, or substantially similar functions or duties for or on behalf of another company for at least 12 months.

(2) The term "company" has the same meaning as in section 202(a)(5) of the Act [15 U.S.C. 80b-2(a)(5)], but does not include a company that is required to be registered under the Investment Company Act of 1940 but is not registered.

(3) The term "private investment company" means a company that would be defined as an investment company under section 3(a) of the Investment Company Act of 1940 [15 U.S.C. 80a-3(a)] but for the exception provided from that definition by section 3(c)(1) of such Act [15 U.S.C. 80a-3(c)(1)].

(4) The term "executive officer" means the president, any vice president in charge of a principal business unit, division or function (such as sales, administration or finance), any other officer who

performs a policy-making function, or any other person who performs similar policy-making functions, for the investment adviser.

(c) Transfer of Management

Limited partners shall have all of the rights afforded shareholders under the Act. If a limited partnership interest is transferred in a manner that is effective under the Partnership Agreement, the transferee shall have all of the rights afforded shareholders under the Act.[27]

4. Transactions with Affiliates

(a) Joint Transactions

A transaction to which a fund, or a company controlled by a fund, and a portfolio affiliate of the fund are parties is exempt from the provisions of section 17(a) of the Act (listing prohibited transactions by affiliated persons and underwriters), provided that none of the following persons is a party to the transaction, or has a direct or indirect financial interest in a party to the transaction other than the fund:

(1) An officer, director, employee, investment adviser, member of an advisory board, depositor, promoter of or principal underwriter for the fund;

(2) A person directly or indirectly controlling the fund;

(3) A person directly or indirectly owning, controlling or holding with power to vote five

---

[27] 17 CFR 270.2a19-2

percent or more of the outstanding voting securities of the fund;

(4) A person directly or indirectly under common control with the fund, other than:

i. A portfolio affiliate of the fund; or

ii. A fund whose sole interest in the transaction or a party to the transaction is an interest in the portfolio affiliate; or

iii. An affiliated person of any of the persons mentioned in paragraphs (a)(1)-(4) of this section, other than the fund or a portfolio affiliate of the fund.[28]

The purchase of a security that is no longer an Eligible Security (as defined in paragraph (a)(10) of § 270.2a-7) from an open-end investment company holding itself out as a "money market" fund shall be exempt from section 17(a) of the Act [15 U.S.C. 80a-17(a)], provided that:

(a) The purchase price is paid in cash; and

(b) The purchase price is equal to the greater of the amortized cost of the security or its market price (in each case, including accrued interest).[29] Brokerage Transactions

(b) Brokerage transactions

§ 270.17e-1 Brokerage transactions on a securities exchange.

For purposes of section 17(e)(2)(A) of the Act [15 U.S.C. 80a-17(e)(2)(A)], a commission, fee or other

---

[28] 17 CFR 270.17a-6

[29] 17 CFR 270.17a-9

remuneration shall be deemed as not exceeding the usual and customary broker's commission, if:

(a) The commission, fee, or other remuneration received or to be received is reasonable and fair compared to the commission, fee or other remuneration received by other brokers in connection with comparable transactions involving similar securities being purchased or sold on a securities exchange during a comparable period of time;

(b) The board of directors, including a majority of the directors of the investment company who are not interested persons thereof:

(1) Has adopted procedures which are reasonably designed to provide that such commission, fee, or other remuneration is consistent with the standard described in paragraph (a) of this section;

(2) Makes and approves such changes as the board deems necessary; and

(3) Determines no less frequently than quarterly that all transactions effected pursuant to this section during the preceding quarter (other than transactions in which the person acting as broker is a person permitted to enter into a transaction with the investment company by § 270.17a-10) were effected in compliance with such procedures;

(c) The board of directors of the investment company satisfies the fund governance standards defined in § 270.0-1(a)(7); and

(d) The investment company:

(1) Shall maintain and preserve permanently in an easily accessible place a copy of the procedures (and any modification thereto) described in paragraph (b)(1) of this section; and

(2) Shall maintain and preserve for a period not less than six years from the end of the fiscal year in which any transactions occurred, the first two years in an easily accessible place, a record of each such transaction (other than any transaction in which the person acting as broker is a person permitted to enter into a transaction with the investment company by § 270.17a-10) setting forth the amount and source of the commission, fee or other remuneration received or to be received, the identity of the person acting as broker, the terms of the transaction, and the information or materials upon which the findings described in paragraph (b)(3) of this section were made.[30]

5.   Sale of Fund Shares

(a)   Disclosure Requirements

Under Section 270.34b-1 of the Investment Company Act of 1940, sales literature (except that of a money market fund) containing a quotation of yield or tax equivalent yield must also contain the total return information. Sales literature cannot be deemed misleading as defined by Section 230.482 of the Investment Company Act of 1940.

An advertisement must include a statement that:

---

[30] 17 CFR 270.17e-1

(i) Advises an investor to consider the investment objectives, risks, and charges and expenses of the investment company carefully before investing; explains that the prospectus contains this and other information about the investment company; identifies a source from which an investor may obtain a prospectus; and states that the prospectus should be read carefully before investing; or

(ii) If used with a Profile, advises an investor to consider the investment objectives, risks, and charges and expenses of the investment company carefully before investing; explains that the accompanying Profile contains this and other information about the investment company; describes the procedures for investing in the investment company; and indicates the availability of the investment company's prospectus.

Additionally, advertisements including performance data must state that the quoted date represents past performance; that past performance does not guarantee future results; that the investment return and principal value of an investment will fluctuate so that an investor's shares, when redeemed, may be worth more or less than their original cost; and that current performance may be lower or higher than the performance data quoted.[31]

(b) Controls on Prices

Some funds have a demand feature which allows the holder of a security to sell the security at an

---

exercise price equal to the approximate amortized cost of the security plus accrued interest, if any, at the time of exercise.[32]

(c) Exchange Traded Funds

An **exchange-traded fund** (or **ETF**) is an investment vehicle traded on stock exchanges, much like stocks. An ETF holds assets such as stocks or bonds and trades at approximately the same price as the net asset value of its underlying assets over the course of the trading day. Most ETFs track an index, such as the Dow Jones Industrial Average or the S&P 500. ETFs may be attractive as investments because of their low costs, tax efficiency, and stock-like features. In a survey of investment professionals conducted in March 2008, 67% called ETFs the most innovative investment vehicle of the last two decades and 60% reported that ETFs have fundamentally changed the way they construct investment portfolios. [1] [2]

An ETF combines the valuation feature of a mutual fund or unit investment trust, which can be purchased or redeemed at the end of each trading day for its net asset value, with the tradability feature of a closed-end fund, which trades throughout the trading day at prices that may be substantially more or less than its net asset value. Closed-end funds are not considered to be exchange-traded funds, even though they are funds and are traded on an exchange. ETFs have been available in the US since 1993 and in Europe since 1999. ETFs traditionally have been index funds, but in 2008 the U.S. Securities and Exchange Commission began to authorize the creation of actively-managed ETFs.[3]

---

[32] 17 CFR 270.2a-7

Most investors can buy and sell ETF shares only in market transactions, but institutional investors can redeem large blocks of shares of the ETF (known as "creation units") for a "basket" of the underlying assets or, alternatively, exchange the underlying assets for creation units. This creation and redemption of shares enables institutions to engage in arbitrage that causes the value of the ETF to approximate the net asset value of the underlying assets.

VIII. SANCTIONS FOR VIOLATIONS

1. SEC Investigations
    The SEC enforces federal securities laws and civil insider trading cases. If the SEC considers criminal prosecution to be appropriate, it refers the case to the US Department of Justice. The SEC can commence an informal inquiry by its enforcement division and does not involve the use of subpoenas. However, formal investigation requires SEC authorization and court enforcement sometimes.

    The SEC can:
    a. Issue cease and desist orders against any person based on any violation of the federal securities laws - The SEC must prove a violation of the securities laws and provide a justifiable explanation why such sanction is appropriate
    b. Levy monetary penalties against regulated persons
    c. Suspend trading in a security on an exchange - not to exceed 10 days
    d. Impose broker/dealer disciplinary sanctions

2. SEC Administrative Proceedings

All formal administrative proceedings before the SEC are conducted in accordance with its Rules of Practice, which must conform to the Administrative Procedure Act which are designed to ensure due process. Reasonable advance notice of the proceeding must be given as well as adequate specification of the charges or issues involved. All parties, including counsel for the interested Division or Office of the Commission, may appear and present evidence and cross-examine witnesses at the hearing in much the same manner as in the trial of court actions. In some cases, in lieu of a formal hearing, the parties may agree to a stipulation of the facts that serves as a record of the proceeding.

Hearings are conducted before a Hearing Officer who is normally an Administrative Law Judge appointed by the Commission; he serves independently of the interested Division or Office and rules on the admissibility of evidence and on other issues arising during the course of the hearing.[33]

3.   SEC Injunctive Actions

The Division of enforcement institutes administrative and injunctive actions. Injunctive actions are brought in either U.S. Federal Court or as an administrative proceeding, heard by an administrative law judge.

4.   Criminal Prosecutions

Violation of Sections 10(b) and 14(e) of the Securities Exchange Act of 1934 can cause insider trading liability. Nearly all criminal insider trading cases also involve mail fraud, wire fraud, tax fraud, perjury, and obstruction of justice.[34] Many times, the SEC pursues both criminal and civil penalties for corporate wrongdoing.[35] A

---

[33] 1-1 Federal Securities Act of 1933 § 1.03

[34] http://www.citeulike.org/user/yanshanxiao/article/3339087

[35] http://www.wilmerhale.com/publications/whPubsDetail.aspx?publication=1513

corporation is liable for the criminal misdeeds of its agents acting within the actual or apparent scope of their employment or authority if the agents intend, at least in part, to benefit the corporation, even though their actions may be contrary to corporate policy or express corporate order. A corporate compliance program, even one specifically prohibiting the very conduct in question, does not absolve the corporation from criminal liability under the doctrine of respondeat superior.

5. SRO Disciplinary Proceedings

Self regulatory organizations (SRO) include the NYSE, Boston Stock Exchange, Chicago Mercantile Exchange, and NASADQ. The Financial Industry Regulatory Authority (FINRA) is a SRO under the Exchange Act of 1934 and is responsible for governing business between brokers, dealers and the investing public. FINRA performs market regulation under contract for The NASDAQ Stock Market, the American Stock Exchange, the International Securities Exchange and the Chicago Climate Exchange.[36]

IX. LIABILITY

1. Sources of Civil Liability

The Insider Trading and Securities Fraud Enforcement Act of 1988 authorizes the SEC to seek a court order imposing a civil penalty on any person who violated the Exchange Act by purchasing or selling securities while in possession of material nonpublic information, or by tipping material nonpublic information to another person who purchased or sold securities while in possession of that information.

---

[36] http://www.finra.org/AboutFINRA/index.htm

In addition, the act provides for the imposition of a civil penalty on any person who directly or indirectly controlled a person who engaged in unlawful trading or tipping, if the controlling person failed to take appropriate steps to prevent the controlled person's violation of law.

The maximum penalty that may be imposed on a controlling person is "the greater of $1,000,000, or three times the amount of the profit gained or loss avoided as a result of [the] controlled person's violation."

2. Jurisdictional Issues

(a) Venue

Section 27 of the Exchange Act is the basis for venue, and states that venue is proper in any district where the defendant "transacts business." 15 U.S.C. § 78aa. However, "[f]or the convenience of the parties and witnesses, in the interest of justice, a district court may transfer any civil action to another district or division where it might have been brought." 28 U.S.C. § 1404(a).[37]

(b) Statute of Limitations

The Investment Advisors Act does not contain a statute of limitations provision. However, a court found in 2007 that the SEC has a five year statute of limitations codified under 28 U.S.C. §2462. Section 2462 is a "catch-all" limitations provision, which states that "an action, suit or proceeding for the enforcement of any civil fine, penalty, or forfeiture, pecuniary or otherwise, shall not be entertained

---

[37] https://ecf.dcd.uscourts.gov/cgi-bin/show_public_doc?2007cv0407-20

unless commenced within five years from the date when the claim first accrued."[38]

3. Plaintiffs

    (a) Class Actions

    A class action lawsuit is where a representative sues on behalf of a group. In order to sue as a class, there must be too many plaintiffs for practical joinder, there must be some questions of law or fact in common to the class, the representative's claims/defenses must be typical of those of the class, and the representative will adequately and fairly represent class.

    (b) Derivative Actions

    A derivative lawsuit occurs when a shareholder brings suit on behalf of the corporation claiming that management breach reduced the residual value of the business. Conversely, a direct suit is a personal claim by a shareholder. The two pronged Tooley test is used to determine whether a suit is direct or derivative. In order for the suit to be derivative, the corporation must have suffered the alleged harm, and the corporation must receive a benefit from recovery.

    Often derivative suits are brought against officers or directors of a corporation for violations of fiduciary duties owed to the shareholders.

    A strike suits occurs when a plaintiff with a relatively small stake in the corporation brings suit with the primary purpose of being bought off.

---

[38] http://www.law.com/jsp/ihc/PubArticleIHC.jsp?id=1177664672451

To prevent abuse of strike suits, states enacted legislation requiring security bond to be posted. States may also restrict derivative suits to shareholders with certain percentage ownership

Demand Requirement
Before a shareholder can bring derivative suit, internal remedies must be sought first (demand). Demand is a shareholder requesting that the board take action on behalf of the corporation. Demand is a barrier to shareholder derivative suits because it gives the board of directors and opportunity to correct it's wrong. Additionally, it insulates the board of directors from harassment by litigating matters clearly within the discretion of the directors and discourages strike suits.

Demand must be made unless excused under the *Aronson* test (Delaware) or *Akers* test (New York).

Under *Aronson* demand is excused (futile) when one part of the Aronson test is met:

i. Plaintiff must allege particularized facts establishing reasonable doubt that board of directors will make an independent and unbiased decision a/b whether or not to assert claim OR:

- Majority of board of directors has material financial/familial interest
- Majority of board of directors incapable of acting independently for some other

      reason such as
      domination or control
- *Underlying transaction* not a valid exercise of business judgment rule

  ii. Plaintiff can allege w/ particularity that the challenged transaction was not a valid exercise of the BJR

See strike suits and percentage ownership above. Additionally, if demand made, then board of directors can either take action or refuse demand

If demand refused, then shareholder has the right to use "tools at hand" to obtain relevant corp. records, reports, etc. reflecting corp. action to determine whether there is basis to assert that demand wrongfully refused

Shareholder must overcome the board of directors' presumption that demand was not wrongfully refused (board of directors' presumption of not bringing lawsuit, not *underlying transaction*)

  a. NOTE: once demand is made, one cannot argue demand was excused (making demand waives arguing that demand excused)

  b. If shareholder overcomes demand by successfully having demand excused, then BOD can create a SLC to determine if action is best interest of the corp. if 2-part test met

    i. Corp. must prove that SLC was independent, acted in GF, and did a reasonable investigation. SLC has the burden.

ii. If the Δ carries the burden, then courts need to determine by applying their own business judgment whether the motion to dismiss should be granted

SLC has burden to prove independence; question of independence hinges on whether SLC would be capable of making a decision w/only the best interests of the corporation in mind. *(In re Oracle—insider trading, Stanford professors on SLC)*

Usual bases for excusing demand as futile:

a. Majority of board has a material interest in challenged transaction
b. Majority of board is dominated or controlled by alleged wrongdoer;
c. Challenged transaction not product of valid business judgment

(i) When majority of present board did not exercise business judgment in challenged transaction because:

- Majority of board that made challenged trans has been replaced by disinterested and independent members
- Where the litigation arises out of some transaction or event not involving a business decision by the board; and
- Where the challenged decision was made by the board of a different corporation

   (ii) Then – look at if, as of time complaint is filed, the board could have property exercised its independent and disinterested business judgment in responding to a demand.

   (iii) If burden satisfied, demand excused.

Demand will almost always be required unless majority of Board is so directly self-interested in the challenged transaction that there is a serious doubt that the BJR would protect the transaction.

Self interest is direct financial interest in challenged transaction

(c) Bars to Recovery

See strike suits and percentage ownership requirements above.

4. Defendants

(a) Liability of Principal

See Section V. 4(b) above

(b) Aiding and Abetting

Unlike criminal law, aiding and abetting is very narrow in securities law. Under Section 10(b) and Rule 10b-5 of the Exchange Act, aiding and abetting claims are not allowed. Additionally, under Section 11 of the Securities Act there is no aiding and abetting liability.

(c) Indemnification and Contribution

The SEC has always opposed corporate indemnification of executives who violate the securities laws. Doing so, reports attorney Amy Corinne Seidel, is against public policy. A series of recent enforcement actions strengthens the SEC's stance. For example, Xerox indemnified its officers for payments they had made to settle the SEC's claim of accounting fraud. The SEC chair criticized the outcome, and the Commission responded with a new policy: settling officers and directors must now represent to the SEC that they are not being indemnified or reimbursed by the company. Even though indemnification was permitted under Lucent's charter documents, the SEC penalized that company when it indemnified its employees in connection with an SEC investigation into accounting practices. Yet the courts do not always agree with this anti-indemnification stance. The Delaware chancery court held that Rite Aid had to continue advancing defense costs to its former CFO, as required under an indemnification agreement, even though the CFO had admitted to wrongdoing and could not be indemnified under the state statute. The court in another recent case required Homestore to indemnify its former officer, asserting that indemnification is necessary to encourage competent people to serve in corporate roles.

Consider state laws and the charter documents. Directors should ascertain whether the governing state laws have permissive or mandatory indemnification provisions and should review the status periodically. Mandatory provisions generally set eligibility requirements, especially for the advancing of expenses. For example, often the indemnified party must certify that the statute has been satisfied and that he or she will repay the expenses if found not to be entitled to the payment. The author notes that directors should also consider whether any facts are known that would preclude indemnification. As a general rule, the company's charter or bylaws can modify a mandatory statutory provision, while permissive indemnification provisions allow each company to decide case-by-case whether to indemnify employees. Evaluate regularly whether changes should be made in the company's charter or bylaws, in light of applicable statutes and court decisions.

5. Damages

Damages Calculation for Section 11 Liability
Top line number = lower of
  i. price paid for security OR
  ii. offering price Second number =
    a. If plaintiff sells before date lawsuit is filed, then use sale price
    b. If plaintiff does not sell security before judgment is entered into the case, use security price as of date lawsuit is filed
    c. If plaintiff sells in between those two dates, then use the higher of (i) the value of the security date lawsuit is filed OR (ii) value when sold

6. Equitable Relief

The last decade has seen tremendous development globally in legislation making directors and officers accountable to regulators and permitting securities class actions by investors whose shares have lost value. Despite loser-pay rules and restrictions on pretrial discovery, legislators seem likely to give investors more remedies. Even civil-law countries are allowing proceedings, frequently after criminal inquiries, with an effect similar to that of class actions. Litigators Gary Gassman and Perry Granof review the expansion of this worldwide enforcement activity against public companies' executives. For example, in Canada, the provincial securities commissions and self-regulatory organizations govern the securities industry. Most suits originate in Ontario, whose statute permits stockholders' class actions against companies, directors and officers, influential persons, and experts for disclosing information that is materially incorrect, incomplete, misleading, or ill-timed. <u>The statutes in almost every province now empower the courts to grant equitable and legal relief from directors' oppressive or prejudicial actions or threats.</u>

X. REGULATIONS

1. State Regulations

Today, all the states have enacted some form of "blue sky" law designed to apply to securities activities within their individual borders. In general, these statutes seek to regulate such activities by one or more of the following routes: "(1) to prohibit fraud in the offer and sale of securities; (2) to require and regulate licensing of investment advisors, broker-dealers, and their agents; (3) to require the registration of securities, and (4) to determine that the securities meet certain standards which are often referred to as 'merit' or 'fair, just, and equitable' standards." [39]

(a) Anti-Fraud Regulations

While the SEC directly, and through its oversight of the NASD and the various Exchanges, is the main enforcer of the nation's securities laws, each individual state has its own securities regulatory body, typically known as the state Securities Commissioner.

---

[39] http://www.lexisnexis.com/lawschool/study/understanding/pdf/SecuritiesCh1.pdf

Most states have left the anti-fraud regulations to the SEC and the various SROs, but do in fact have the power and authority to bring actions against securities violators pursuant to state law. Further, each state has its own securities act, which governs, at least, the registration and reporting requirements for broker-dealers and stock brokers doing business, sometimes even indirectly, in the state.

The various state securities regulators have most of their impact in the area of registration of securities brokers and dealers, and in the registration of securities transactions. For further information on the state regulatory scheme, and its impact on market participants, see the section on Blue Sky Laws.

(b) Broker-Dealer Registration

Under Section 15 of the Securities Exchange Act of 1934, most "brokers" and "dealers" must register with the SEC and join a "self-regulatory organization," or SRO.

Section 3(4) of the Act defines "broker" broadly as:

> "any person engaged in the business of effecting transactions in securities for the account of others . . . "

The term "person" includes entities as well as individuals.

Unlike a broker who acts as agent, a dealer acts as principal. Section 3(a)(5) of the Act generally defines a "dealer" as:

"any person engaged in the business of buying and selling securities for his own account, through a broker or otherwise . . . "

Traders are excluded from the definition of dealer. A trader is someone who buys and sells securities, either individually or in a trustee capacity, but not as part of a regular business. Individuals who buy and sell securities for themselves generally are considered traders and not dealers.

Sometimes you can easily tell if someone is a broker or dealer. For example, a person who executes transactions for others on a securities exchange clearly is a broker. And a firm that advertises publicly it makes a market in securities is obviously a dealer. Other situations can be less clear.

Please note that special provisions apply to broker and dealer activity by banks. For more information, please see guidance for Banks and Other Depository Institutions.

(c) Registration of Securities

It is important to keep in mind that before a security is sold in a state, there must be a registration in place to cover the transaction, and, the brokerage firm, and the stock broker, must each be registered in the state, or otherwise exempt from the registration requirements.

With few exceptions, every offer or sale of a security must, before it is offered or sold in a state, be registered or exempt from registration under the securities, or blue sky laws, of the state(s) in which the security is offered and sold. Similarly, every brokerage firm, every issuer selling its own securities and an individual broker or issuer representative (i.e., finder) engaged in selling securities in a state, must also be registered in the state, or otherwise exempt from such registration requirements. Most states securities laws are modeled after the Uniform Securities Act of 1956 ("USA"). To date, approximately 40 states use the USA as the basis for their state blue sky laws.

However, although most blue sky laws are modeled after the USA, blue sky statutes vary widely and there is very little uniformity among state securities laws. Therefore, it is vital that each state's statutes and regulations be reviewed before embarking upon any securities sales activities in a state to determine what is permitted, or not permitted, in a particular state. To make matters more complicated, while some states may have identical statutory language or regulations covering particular activities or conduct, their interpretation may differ dramatically from state to state. However, state Securities Commission staff are available to assist in answering questions regarding particular statutory provisions or regulations.

Fortunately, many types of securities, and many transactions in securities, are exempt from state securities registration requirements. For example, many states provide for transactional exemptions for Regulation D private offerings, provided there is full compliance with SEC Rules 501-503. However, through certain types of offerings or transactions may not require registration, many states require filings or place additional conditions on exemptions available for many different offerings for which exemptions are available. The best advice, then, is before offering any security for sale in any state, experienced Blue Sky counsel should be retained to review the applicable state blue sky laws and take any action necessary to permit the offering to be made in the particular state.

The National Securities Markets Improvement Act of 1996 ("NSMIA") was enacted in October, 1996 in response to the states' failure to uniformly regulate certain types of national securities offerings. Among other changes, NSMIA amended Section 18 of the Securities Act of 1933, as amended (the "Act"), thereby creating a class of securities - referred to as "covered securities" - the offer and sale of which (through licensed broker-dealers) are no longer subject to state securities law registration requirements. Covered securities include: securities listed (or approved for listing) on the NYSE, AMEX and the Nasdaq/National Market, and securities of the same issuer which are equal in rank or senior to such listed securities; mutual fund shares; securities sold to certain qualified purchasers (as yet not defined by the SEC); certain securities exempt under Section 3(a) of the Act (including government or municipal securities, bank securities and commercial paper); and securities exempt from registration under the Act if sold in transactions complying with Rule 506 of Regulation D under the Act. Although NSMIA preempts state securities registration requirements, NSMIA preserves the right of the states to investigate and prosecute fraud.

As a result of NSMIA, states may no longer require the registration of covered securities; however, states may, as permitted under NSMIA, require filings and the payment of fees for offers and sales in their state of covered securities other than those which are listed (or approved for listing) on the designated exchanges or securities senior to such securities (i.e.; preferred shares or debt securities of an issuer with common stock listed on the designated exchanges). Additionally, since NSMIA only preempts state securities registration requirements, broker-dealer and agent/salesperson registration requirements (applicable to individuals engaged in the offer and sale of covered securities) must still be examined to determine whether action is required to be taken in connection with a particular offering or transaction. Therefore, although covered securities are no longer subject to substantive state review, blue sky action with respect to offerings of covered securities is still necessary.

(d) Sanctions for Violations

The Sarbanes-Oxley Act of 2002 creates civil and criminal remedies to vindicate employees suffering adverse job actions because of their assistance in investigating an employer's perceived violations of securities and other laws. Attorneys Fred Alvarez and Michael Nader outline the civil provisions, which protect employees (including executives, directors, and officers), contractors, agents, and subcontractors of a public company. The law prohibits the employer from discriminating against whistleblowing employees by threat, harassment, demotion, or discharge, if the whistleblower provides information or otherwise assists in the investigation of what the employee reasonably believes is a violation of the securities laws, SEC regulations, or laws and regulations prohibiting fraud on shareholders. To be protected, the employee must furnish the information or assistance to a federal agency, a member or committee of Congress, the employee's supervisor, or the employer's designee for investigating internal misconduct. The authors indicate early disagreement between the executive and legislative branches over whether the law covers information provided when no one has yet begun or proposed an investigation.

Sarbanes-Oxley's principal enforcement process is administrative. The employee must file a complaint with the Department of Labor, which establishes evidentiary hurdles at the filing and investigative stages. The employee must state a prima facie case, and the employer may present a compelling defense that the unfavorable action would have occurred even without the employee's protected conduct. If the whistleblower's complaint survives and succeeds, the DOL can order the employer to take remedial action, chiefly reinstatement with back pay and interest. The employer may request a hearing and appeal unfavorable rulings to the US Court of Appeals. While Sarbanes-Oxley does not authorize punitive damages, the authors point out, the standard remedies include back pay, seniority, costs, attorneys' and experts' fees, and expunging of negative references in the employee's employment files. The Act also provides criminal sanctions for a knowing interference with anyone's employment for providing information to federal law enforcement authorities investigating any federal criminal offense (a narrower class of recipients but a much broader class for the type of proceedings and the persons protected).

Sarbanes-Oxley assigns responsibility to the public company's audit committee for overseeing the internal complaint process relating to charges affecting the integrity of financial reporting. The SEC has thus far not mandated specific procedures, but the Act provides that whatever procedures are used must ensure anonymity. The authors caution that the procedures a company adopts should focus equally on the prevention of retaliatory conduct that might invoke the protective whistleblower provisions. Employers should, they note, also be aware that state law provisions may apply to close perceived loopholes in the federal protection coverage.[40]

(e) Civil Liabilities

Civil Liabilities Arising in Connection with Prospectuses and Communications

    a. **In general**

Any person who--

1. offers or sells a security in violation of section 5, or

2. offers or sells a security (whether or not exempted by the provisions of section 3, other than paragraphs (2) and (14) of subsection (a) of said section), by the use of any means or instruments of transportation or communication in interstate commerce or of the mails, by means of a prospectus or oral communication, which includes an untrue statement of a material fact or omits to state a material fact necessary in order to make the statements, in the light of the circumstances under which they were made, not misleading (the purchaser not knowing of such untruth or omission), and who shall not sustain the burden of proof that he did not know, and in the exercise of reasonable care could not have known, of such untruth or omission,

---

[40] Abstracted from *ALI-ABA Business Law Course Materials Journal*, published by ALI-ABA Committee on Continuing Professional Education, 4025 Chestnut Street, Philadelphia, PA 19104 3099.

shall be liable, subject to subsection (b), to the person purchasing such security from him, who may sue either at law or in equity in any court of competent jurisdiction, to recover the consideration paid for such security with interest thereon, less the amount of any income received thereon, upon the tender of such security, or for damages if he no longer owns the security.

b. **Loss causation**

In an action described in subsection (a)(2), if the person who offered or sold such security proves that any portion or all of the amount recoverable under subsection (a)(2) represents other than the depreciation in value of the subject security resulting from such part of the prospectus or oral communication, with respect to which the liability of that person is asserted, not being true or omitting to state a material fact required to be stated therein or necessary to make the statement not misleading, then such portion or amount, as the case may be, shall not be recoverable.

(f) Jurisdictional Questions (Cyberspace)[41]
The term "cyberspace," coined by science-fiction writer William Gibson, refers to a "virtual" world quite similar to, and yet entirely unlike, any physical world. Currently, the online world is focused on the Internet, but whatever the regime, the new information environment is <u>moving so quickly</u> that law is wholly unable to keep pace. Searching in the Lexis' "Mega/Mega" database simply for the word

---

[41] This section excerpted from Alex H. Benn's *Law and Finance in the Digital Domain*

"Internet" yielded only 12 cases, with the majority of those only peripherally related to "cyber" issues. In large part, no law adequately precedes or addresses many of the issues. The law has never been good at quick response to shifting technology, and this technology appears to be so revolutionary as to have completely overwhelmed the legal system. Where law is being made, it relies heavily on analogy to other media, and often results in unsound outcomes.

A First Amendment exercise. There are currently many controversies brewing in the First Amendment arena regarding the online world. Discussions often center on the nature of the forum, the "participants," etc. While these are vital issues, they are beyond the scope of this e-paper.

Online securities law issues are only slowly developing. For the most part, action has revolved around online permutations of traditional securities fraud schemes. In investigating the few truly "cyber" cases for an indication of the law of electronic securities information *distribution*, I could only find two recent cases that might have some peripheral relation.

U.S. v. David LaMacchia, 871 F.Supp 535 (1995).

In this case, Mr. LaMacchia, a 21 year old MIT student, was indicted by a grand jury for one count of violating the wire fraud statute, (18 U.S.C. § 1343). I describe the case only briefly, but there is an excellent chronology of the full proceedings available on the Web. Mr. LaMacchia stood accused of running a site at MIT, accessible via the Internet, where copyrighted software materials were improperly available. Damages of over one million dollars had been alleged. Judge Stearns, in dismissing the case, noted that although the copyright violations would indeed be reprehensible, the wire fraud statute was inapplicable to such a case. In discussing the wire fraud statute, he noted that they had been enacted "to cure a jurisdictional defect" (871 F.Supp at 540, 541) created by the emergence of the new media of TV and radio, but that the statute did not extend to this case of Internet copyright violation. In this respect, new legislation may be needed to address the online world.

U.S. v. Thomas (6th Circuit, pending).

This case has generated considerable controversy in the online community. The Thomases, a Milpitas, *California* couple, were convicted *in Tennessee* for conspiring to distribute pornographic material via a computer network. The Thomases operated a computer bulletin board called "Amateur Action" which contained electronic images of many types of pornography. What made the case interesting was that they were convicted in Memphis based on the access available in Tennessee. While much has been written about the "community standards" and First Amendment precedent set by such a ruling, it seems likely that the decision will not stand long.

Though many in the cybercommunity have been up in arms over the potential application of "community standards" at a distance, the case seems to stand more for the hazards of grossly inadequate representation rather than any overarching First Amendment principles. Stanford affiliate Tom Nolan has since taken on the Thomases' appeal. Mr. Williams, the Thomases' trial lawyer, has been reproached by several judges in front of whom he has practiced, including District Judges Aguilar, Ware, and Patel, who contributed a scathing comment while referring Mr. Williams to the state bar for his ineptitude.

Direct Jurisdictional Means

All of this speculation may be irrelevant, because the SEC has already successfully asserted jurisdiction over securities matters when only the most tenuous of interstate facilities are used. Where there is fraud, the SEC has very broad construction over the jurisdictional bases of its statutes: "That the jurisdictional hook need not be large to fish for securities law violations is well established."[1]. In addition to the mail and wire fraud statutes, the '33 and '34 Acts are littered with jurisdictional "hooks." Section 5 speaks of "...any means or instruments of transportation or communication in interstate commerce...," and § 17 speaks in similar terms regarding fraud in offers and sales.

Seligman and Loss note that "it now seems fairly clear that the jurisdictional base of the section [§ 5] could be constitutionally expanded so that it would apply to all steps in the process of selling -- from offer to delivery and payment -- if the mails or interstate facilities were used in any one step."[2] The authors also note that it is well-settled that even intrastate phone calls are sufficient to invoke jurisdiction [3], and that there is "nothing in the context or background of the Act to suggest a grudging construction of the jurisdictional language."[4]

With all this as background, I can offhand envision several potential areas for interesting speculation. First, the Internet is arguably an entirely privatized body in the United States, potentially exempt from the same restrictions applicable to a regulated national phone or mail system. I doubt that this position would be availing in the end, though. Secondly, it could be argued, much like the LaMacchia case, that the current instrumentalities were unimagined when the Securities Acts were drawn up, and thus could not have been included within the ambit of construction. Again, I find this argument unpersuasive and believe that communications traveling over the Internet, relating to the offering and sale of securities in the United States, would be encompassed within the SEC's jurisdiction. Thirdly, one might speculate on the status of a foreign issuer "serving-up" documents from outside the U.S. with the recognition that U.S. citizens would purchase their securities. This scenario, while fascinating, is beyond the scope of this paper, and is at this juncture wholly speculative. Finally, on a more micro level, one might wonder whether the oral offers permitted in intrastate telephone calls during the waiting period would analogize to written or oral e-mail offers, but this issue currently remains merely a topic of speculation and lobbying. Many other related issues revolve around this introduction of new communication technology into the information distribution process, but it simply appears to be too early to predict how events will shake out.

The SEC Sidles toward Cyberspace
The Clinton/Gore administration has clearly been able to watch its vision of an online government begin to take shape around them, though it remains debatable to what extent the administration has helped or hindered the efforts. As I note in the information distribution portion of the paper, major federal agencies are establishing online presences at a staggering rate. The SEC, however is remarkable in its absence. Even the admirable EDGAR project is being provided to the Internet from outside the agency itself. Although I understand that there are "policy groups" within the agency studying various "cyberissues," there has been precious little information leaked to the

outside world about the status or direction of these projects. Thus far in the Internet era, there have been two major securities law developments.

Witbeer - The First "Internet IPO"

Spring Street Brewery, a New York microbrewery, gained recognition as the first company to "go public" on the Internet. It is now possible to download a copy of their offering circular from their Web site. I spoke with the president of the company, Mr. Andrew Klein, a Harvard Law School graduate and Cravath, Swaine & Moore alumnus, and he explained that the company is making use of the Regulation A exemption to offer less than $5 million worth of securities without any prohibition on general solicitations. It would seem that one could do a Rule 504 Regulation D offering in a similar manner, but with a restriction to $1M of securities.

Mr. Klein stated that the company is promoting the offering via several channels, and is currently receiving funds at a proportion of 25% from the Internet, 50% from paid advertisement (including point-of-sale ads), and 25% from the general media. He has had over 500,000 visitors to the web site, and the offering circular has only been available since February, 1995. The offering circular was not posted to the web site prior to its qualification by the SEC.

During the comment process, the SEC seemed to concentrate on the fact that by visiting the page before downloading the prospectus, there would be additional writings communicated *prior* to receipt of the final offering circular. However, Mr. Klein managed to analogize the web page to a cover letter sent with a prospectus, and this satisfied the SEC's concerns. More difficult has been compliance with the multitude of state regimes. Currently, the web page lists in which of the states the offering is legal, and in which it is working to secure approval, but of course the circular may be downloaded from any state in the country. There are additional representations required of purchasers upon subscription, but it remains an open question whether the offering is violating various state laws by making an improper offering in their jurisdiction. A fair analogy is to a tombstone in the Wall Street Journal, which will appear in states where offerings are not qualified, but this does not answer the question of the circular itself appearing in states where it is not qualified. At bottom, however, although this action is potentially illegal, state regulators have better fish to fry. To date, Mr. Klein has not heard any complaints from state securities regulators on this issue.

This type of "small-fry" offering may become useful to small companies that wish to raise capital without the burden of underwriting fees. It will be interesting to note how this area develops. In an article describing the Witbeer offering, John Heine, a spokesman for the U.S. Securities and Exchange Commission, was quoted as saying that the agency hadn't issued any rules regarding electronic investment.[5] , but Mr. Klein noted that the examiners he dealt with in qualifying his offering stated that there were definitely groups within the SEC studying the issues. I attempted to pierce the veil of the SEC to locate any of these groups for comment, but was unsuccessful in my efforts.

The Brown & Wood No-Action Letter

On the other end of the size spectrum is the Brown & Wood no action letter, dealing with prospectus distribution in a more traditional broker/underwriter setting. For your reference, I provide "highlighted" versions of both the underline original underline query and the underline SEC's response underline. Although an underline article in the Wall Street Letter underline states that the letter was the result of underline eight months underline of negotiation, it is still a rather tentative step in the direction of electronic distribution.

Brown & Wood submitted the request for interpretation on behalf of clients Merrill Lynch and Goldman Sachs. Essentially, the problem sought to be solved is the pressure to deal with the T+3 settlement requirements in light of § 5(b)(2) requirement to deliver a final § 2(10) prospectus prior to delivery of other writings (so as not to render the other writings also a prospectus). In response to a detailed and well-argued no-action request by Brown & Wood, the SEC issued underline nine specific guidelines underline addressing concerns raised by electronic distribution of prospectuses. At their core, these prescriptions boil down to issues of access, insuring that investors will not receive any less information or choice than they already enjoy under a paper-based prospectus distribution regime. In an underline article for the Institutional Investor underline, Abigail Arms of the SEC was quoted as saying that any issuer or underwriter could rely on the ruling. While definitely a move in the right direction, underline the ruling raises more questions than it answers underline, and takes too small a step in sanctioning true electronic distribution.

2. Regulation of Cross-Border Securities Transactions[42]

---

[42] This section excerpted from a speech given by Erik R. Sirri, Director, Division of Market Regulation, U.S. Securities and Exchange Commission, in Boston, MA, on March 1, 2007

By Erik R. Sirri

**Director, Division of Market Regulation
U.S. Securities and Exchange Commission**

*Boston, Massachusetts
March 1, 2007*

Thank you. At the outset, let me remind you that the views I express are my own and not necessarily the views of the Commission, the individual Commissioners, or my colleagues on the Commission staff.

Today, I will address the increasing pace of cross-border securities transactions. More companies are raising capital beyond their geographic boundaries. U.S. investors are allocating their capital in foreign securities markets at a higher rate, and our securities markets have attracted an increasing share of foreign investments. It is important that our regulatory system not only continue to keep pace, but also facilitate the benefits of a global market place. So, I will share with you some of my views on the issue. I will propose a solution to remove from our securities markets possible frictions that do not serve to protect investors or facilitate capital formation and that may be unnecessary to maintain fair, orderly, and efficient markets.

The SEC may use its exemptive authority, provided that it can make the requisite findings, to eliminate frictions that do not further our goals. At the same time, however, the SEC cannot abdicate its obligation to protect investors and further market integrity.

Introduction: The Issue
The financial services industry is a large segment of our economy. It contributed $957.7 billion to U.S. Gross Domestic Product in 2005, or about 7.7 percent of total GDP.[2] The securities industry employs nearly 800,000

people. That is over 200,000 people more than the total population of Boston or Washington, DC. Indeed, it is a key component of the U.S. economy.

There has been a great deal of growth in the demand to trade securities. According to a joint report by the Investment Company Institute and the Securities Industry and Financial Markets Association, the number of households owning equities has increased more than three-fold since the early 1980s. Half of U.S. households, nearly 57 million, own stocks directly or through mutual funds. By comparison, approximately 40 million households viewed last week's Academy Awards. Two-thirds of all equity investors in 2005 were in their peak earning and investing years - ages of 35 and 64.

U.S. investors have an equity culture, as evidenced by their willingness to invest in mutual funds, equities, and exchange traded funds. This makes them attractive customers, both for U.S. and for foreign financial service providers.

The daily volume at the New York Stock Exchange has grown exponentially, from approximately 40 million shares in the 1980s to over 3 billion shares in recent times. The NASDAQ has also seen its daily trading volume soar past the 3 billion shares mark.

Demand has risen across the board (institutional and retail) as transactions costs have fallen. Institutional trading costs appear to have declined by about 23 basis points (roughly 5 cents per share) after the securities markets shifted in 2000 from trading in fractions, to trading in pennies - an average monthly savings of about $133 million in institutional trading costs. The switch to decimals reduced the minimum "spread" or gap between buy and sell prices from 1/16 - the equivalent of 6.25 cents - to a penny.

The SEC has had a fundamental role in the growth of the financial services markets - while working to maintain the integrity and vitality of the markets and protecting the interests of investors. Examples of regulatory changes that have facilitated innovation in the financial services markets include: the order handling rules, which cleared the way for electronic markets, best execution obligations, pennies in equities, penny pilot in options, Regulation NMS, and TRACE.

Order Handling Rules. In 1996, the SEC adopted a rule requiring the display of customer limit orders and amended the rule governing publication of quotations to enhance the quality of published quotations for securities and to enhance competition and pricing efficiency in the markets. The Limit Order Display Rule requires that limit orders be displayed when they are priced better than, or add to the size associated with, quotes posted by the specialist or market makers. The rule allows the general public to compete directly with professional market participants in the quote-setting process. The Quote Rule requires a market maker to publicly display their most competitive quotes. This rule gives the public access to quotes posted by market makers in Electronic Communication Networks (ECN). For example, if a dealer places a limit order into an ECN, the price and quantity are incorporated in the ECN quote displayed on NASDAQ if it represents the best bid or offer in ECN.

The display and quote rules fueled the rise of the ECNs. At the same time, the order handling rules benefit investors by increasing transparency in those markets and improving opportunities for the best execution of customer orders.

Decimalization. In June 2000, the SEC issued an order directing NASD and the national securities exchanges to act jointly in developing a plan to convert their quotations in equity securities and options from fractions to decimals (decimalization). The markets chose to trade equities in pennies. Many proponents of decimalization anticipated that penny prices would reduce trading costs for investors by, among other things, permitting quotation spreads (the difference between the highest bid quotation and the lowest offer quotation) to narrow from the 1/16th minimum increment that was standard in the fractional environment. Early studies by the SEC's Office of Economic Analysis (OEA) and NASDAQ indicated that there was significant narrowing of quotation spreads. OEA estimated, for example, that from December 2000 to March 2001, quotation spreads in securities listed on the New York Stock Exchange narrowed an average of 37%, and effective spreads narrowed 15%. The same studies observed even greater impact on NASDAQ securities, with spreads narrowing an average of 50% following decimalization, and effective spreads narrowing almost as much.

Penny Pilot in Options. The SEC also has encouraged a pilot for exchanges to quote certain series of option classes in penny increments. As of February 9th, options in 12 classes that are priced below $3 are quoted in pennies; options in those 12 classes priced $3 and above are quoted in nickels. And all series of the QQQQ are quoted in pennies. The exchanges and the SEC plan to closely examine the impact of these smaller increments on market quality and options system capacity. Preliminary indications are that spreads have narrowed, but the SEC staff has not yet analyzed whether there are differences in the benefits depending on the price and trading volume of the option.

Also worth noting is that all of the options exchanges have reduced or eliminated the fees they collected from market makers for use in paying for order flow for the 13 options classes in the penny pilot. This response is consistent with what we saw when stocks started trading in pennies.

Regulation NMS. In 2005, the SEC adopted Regulation NMS, for National Market System. It is intended to modernize and strengthen the markets for equity securities by requiring markets to protect best quotes of automated markets. This has prompted tremendous innovation in our markets. Shortly after the adoption of Regulation NMS, traditional markets intensified their strategic process of modernization. The New York Stock Exchange merged with the fully automated Arca Exchange, and initiated a move to a hybrid electronic-floor based trading system. Similarly, NASDAQ has merged with Inet, registered as an exchange, and adopted the Inet trading technology as its trading platform. The Amex is transforming its traditional floor-based market to a hybrid market that offers fully automated trading.

TRACE. In 1998, then SEC Chairman Levitt called for, and in 2001 the SEC approved, the first major transparency initiative in the corporate bond markets, in which the NASD mandated that all dealers and inter-dealers report the prices of corporate bond trades to its Trade Reporting and Compliance Engine (TRACE). Some of the expected benefits from the increased transparency include: increased market efficiency; better risk and portfolio management; sophisticated trading strategies; better valuation models; new market participants; deterrent to improper trade practices; and enhanced technology. The MSRB committed to implementing trade reporting requirements in 1994, a process that culminated in January 2005 with "real-time" trade reporting for municipal securities.

The changes in rules have unleashed the winds of change in the markets, driven by the revolution in technology and falling prices of communication technology, has affected the markets in profound ways. At the same time, there has been a lot of activity in the exchange space.

We have had new market centers: International Stock Exchange, Boston Options Exchange, and now BATS, which began trading in January 2006. The NYSE plans to introduce a new corporate bond trading platform - NYSE | Bonds, using the technology of the NYSE Arca all-electronic trading platform, which aims to provide a more efficient and transparent way to trade corporate bonds. The Chicago Board Options Exchange, the largest U.S. options exchange, recently launched its own stock exchange.

Exchanges have demutualized and become for-profit. In 2005, approximately 213 years after its founding, the NYSE went public. The Chicago Board of Trade went public in October 2005, 157 years after it opened its doors for business. The century old Chicago Mercantile Exchange took the same step in 2002. NASDAQ also went public in 2002, 31 years after its founding.

Like all growing business areas, U.S. financial service providers are looking for alliances, both domestically and abroad.

Exchanges have been joining forces through alliances and mergers.

- NASDAQ bought a 15 percent stake in the London Stock Exchange, and subsequently raised its stake to just below 30 percent in a failed takeover bid.

- The NYSE reached agreement to merge with pan-European stock and derivatives exchange Euronext in a deal that will create the first trans-Atlantic equities market.

- The Chicago Mercantile Exchange reached agreement to buy cross-town rival CBOT to create the world's largest publicly traded futures exchange by market cap.

- The NYSE formed a strategic alliance with the Tokyo Stock Exchange to develop and study opportunities in trading systems and technology, investment products and governance. Less than a month later, the Tokyo Stock Exchange and the London Stock Exchange announced that they would work together to share technology information and possibly develop new products.

- The NYSE agreed to buy a 5-percent interest in the National Stock Exchange of India Ltd. in Mumbai for $115 million in cash.

Technology has changed the global playing field for broker-dealers as well, as it has reduced the communication barriers that once separated markets. As U.S. institutions' appetite for foreign securities has grown, so has the global reach of securities firms. U.S. "bulge bracket" firms have developed a multinational footprint, with operations that span the globe. There has been cross-border consolidation among broker-dealers as well.

- Credit Suisse Group, a financial services company headquartered in Zürich, Switzerland, purchased First Boston in 1988. The firm later merged with Donaldson, Lufkin, & Jenrette.

- Deutsche Bank AG with headquarters located in Frankfurt, Germany, acquired Bankers Trust in 1998, thereby acquiring the 200 year-old U.S. investment bank Alex. Brown & Sons.

- In 2000, another Swiss financial services company, UBS AG, a financial services company, headquartered in Basel and Zürich, Switzerland, purchased U.S. brokerage firm PaineWebber Inc.

In addition, foreign financial services companies have been increasingly reaching out to U.S. institutions pursuant to conditional exemptions from broker-dealer registration. But as the ease at dealing from overseas with U.S. persons has grown, and regulatory oversight in foreign jurisdictions has evolved, foreign securities firms and markets have inquired about access to U.S. markets without U.S. regulation, based on the nature and quality of their supervision. I believe the time has come to reconsider our approach and to allow access under conditions that protect U.S. investors and maintain the integrity of U.S. markets.

In this talk I will flesh this out for you, first detailing where we stand today in terms of allowing foreign exchanges and foreign broker-dealers to operate in the U.S.

Background: How Our Markets Are Regulated Today
There is not time here for a course on securities regulation, but the basic frame work for securities law is pretty straightforward. For our purposes, it is enough to think of the three actors who are involved in this space: corporate issuers, securities exchanges, and broker-dealers.

The federal securities laws are concerned with both the initial distribution of securities, and their subsequent trading. The securities laws afford investors broad protection through disclosure and anti-fraud provisions. In particular, the securities laws and SEC rules prohibit fraudulent activities by any person that defraud investors in the U.S., regardless of how novel or complex the scheme, or country of origin. Provisions in the securities laws prohibit certain types of trading activity outright, such as insider trading and market manipulation.

Under the Securities Act, securities that are offered to the public must be registered with the SEC by the issuer, or be exempt from registration. Securities offered privately to sophisticated investors need not be registered. Also, securities offered offshore need not be registered. In addition, the Exchange Act addresses the post-distribution period, that is, subsequent trading. Generally speaking, an issuer must register securities under the Exchange Act the first time that it has 500 shareholders of record in a class of equity securities and ten million dollars in total assets. An issue must also be registered if listed on an exchange operating in the U.S. Foreign issuers with requisite U.S. shareholders need not register if they are not traded on an exchange or an automated interdealer quotation system in the U.S. Thus, issuers become reporting companies as a result of either of the following: (1) registration of an offering of securities pursuant to the Securities Act, or (2) registration of a class of securities under the Exchange Act. The principal reports required to be filed with the SEC by reporting companies include the annual report on Form 10-K; the quarterly report on Form 10-Q; and current report on Form 8-K. These forms require, among other things, that financial information comply with GAAP rules, or for foreign issuers, reconciliation to U.S. GAAP. The Securities Act and the Exchange Act subject the issuer, its officers and directors, as well as its underwriters to civil and criminal liability.

The Securities Act, at times referred as the "truth in securities" law, has two basic objectives:

>(1) require that investors receive financial and other significant information concerning securities being offered for public sale; and

>(2) prohibit deceit, misrepresentations, and other fraud in the sale of securities.

A primary means of accomplishing these goals is the disclosure of important financial information through the registration of securities. This information enables investors to make informed judgments about whether to purchase a company's securities. For this reason, a

U.S. securities exchange cannot trade the shares of a foreign corporation unless those shares are registered in the U.S. and comparable periodic disclosure is filed.

Some foreign issuers have registered their shares with the SEC. But other major global firms have not.

The second group of players is the exchanges. The first thing to realize is that with the exception of a few exchanges, most trading done outside of the U.S. is electronic, and access to those exchanges is via a trading screen. Hence, the physical location of an exchange becomes an elusive concept, and what counts is the domicile of the exchange for regulatory and business purposes.

The statutory definition of "exchange" includes a "market place or facilities for bringing together purchasers and sellers of securities or for otherwise performing with respect to securities the functions commonly performed by a stock exchange." Rule 3b-16 under the Exchange Act interprets what is meant by this phrase. That is, one maintains a market place or facility, or otherwise performs functions commonly performed by a stock exchange if one: (1) brings together the orders of multiple buyers and sellers; and (2) uses established, non-discretionary methods (whether by providing a trading facility or by setting rules) under which such orders interact with each other, and the buyers and sellers entering such orders agree to the terms of a trade.

Every market that meets the definition of "exchange" under the Exchange Act must either register as a national securities exchange or be exempted from registration on the basis of limited transaction volume or as an alternative trading system. To be exempt as an alternative trading system, the system must not act as a self-regulatory organization or call itself an exchange. Congress gave the exchanges the obligation to enforce their members' compliance with the federal securities laws and, in 1983, required every broker-dealer to become a member of an exchange or a securities association. Direct access to exchanges is limited to registered broker-dealers. Every registered exchange is required to assist the SEC in assuring fair and orderly markets, to have effective mechanisms for enforcing the securities laws and regulation, and to submit their rules to the SEC for review.

The SEC is charged with helping to promote investor protection, to ensure fair and orderly markets, to prevent fraud and manipulation, and to promote market coordination and competition for the benefit of all investors. Congress decided that these goals should be achieved primarily through the regulation of exchanges and through authority it granted to the SEC in the 1975 Amendments, to adopt rules that promote (1) economically efficient execution of securities transactions, (2) fair competition, (3) transparency, (4) investor access to the best markets, and (5) the opportunity for investors' orders to be executed without the participation of a dealer.

Our national market system for U.S. registered stocks, as it has evolved since 1975, has sought the benefits both of market centralization, which enhances depth and liquidity in the markets, and competition. The SEC has sought to maintain this balance through a market system marked by balanced regulation, with individual markets that are linked together to make their best prices publicly known and accessible.

The Exchange Act requires registered exchanges and securities associations to consider the public interest in administering their markets, to allocate reasonable fees equitably, and to establish rules designed to admit members fairly. The Exchange Act also requires registered exchanges and securities associations to establish rules that assure fair representation of members and investors in selecting directors and administering their organizations.

Self-Regulation. Exchanges and securities associations such as the NASD act as SROs and, as such, are required not only to comply with the Exchange Act, but also to carry out the purposes of the Exchange Act. They do this principally by enforcing member compliance with the provisions of the Exchange Act and the rules promulgated thereunder, as well as with the rules of the exchanges or the associations. This system requires exchanges and securities associations to establish rules and procedures to prevent fraud and manipulation and promote just and equitable principles of trade, typically by establishing audit trails, surveillance, and disciplinary programs.

With respect to market operations, a registered exchange adopts rules governing all aspects of trading on its market, including the manner in which trading interest is displayed and orders interact. These rules must treat all market participants - particularly public customers - fairly and equitably, and refrain from imposing any unnecessary or inappropriate burdens on competition.

In addition, a registered exchange must adopt appropriate listing standards for its listed companies, and have rules assuring that transactions on the exchange participate efficiently and effectively in the clearance and settlement process. With respect to member regulation, a registered exchange must have a wide range of rules that assure appropriate member conduct, sales practices (including rules that require members to obtain best execution of customer orders and the suitability of recommended transactions), financial responsibility, supervision, disciplinary proceedings, education and training. Registered exchanges are required to surveil vigorously their markets for inappropriate conduct, and their members for violations of their rules and the federal securities laws and rules, and to take appropriate disciplinary action. In this regard, exchanges provide the first line of defense in the enforcement of the U.S. regime of securities regulation. Without the benefit of self-regulation by the exchanges, the SEC's oversight of the U.S. markets would be reduced.

Continuity of Market Operations. U.S. exchanges are required to maintain sufficient systems capacity to handle foreseeable trading volume. In addition, exchanges must maintain appropriate computer system integrity and security to operate a market. To this end, exchanges must submit systems changes that are rules of the exchange to the SEC for review. The failure of a market to maintain systems in compliance with SEC standards would jeopardize its ability to remain operational during periods of market stress.

Price Transparency. Registered exchanges are required to disseminate real-time trade and quotation information to the public through joint participation in market-wide quotation and transaction reporting plans. This consolidation of market information is a critical component of the U.S. national market system, as the resulting price transparency promotes efficient price discovery and helps assure best execution of customer orders. The exclusion of a market from the consolidated data stream would impair transparency and price discovery for U.S. investors.

Fair Access and Fair Competition. All registered exchanges must accept all qualified US broker-dealers as members, have fair membership standards, not unfairly deny persons access to their trading or other facilities, and equitably allocate reasonable fees and other charges among their members These safeguards help assure that competition among US markets and market participants will be vigorous but fair. If a market was not subject to these requirements, it could unfairly discriminate or deny access to a U.S. broker-dealer and compete unfairly with U.S. exchanges.

Rule Filing Process. Registered exchanges are required to file rule changes with the SEC that encompass all material aspects of trading on their markets and regulation of their members. The notice, public comment, and SEC review process that is associated with this rule filing requirement is the primary means through which the SEC determines whether exchanges are designed to fulfill their critical self-regulatory functions discussed above. Markets operated in the U.S. without being subject to this requirement would deprive U.S. investors the benefit of SEC oversight and public comment in this process.

Exchanges not registered in the United States may not be required provide many of these protections, especially provisions that seek to prevent fraud or manipulation. So U.S. investors might not be protected from insider trading, front running, trading ahead, etc.

Briefly, today no foreign exchange can put one of their trading screens in the U.S. unless it registers under Section 6 of the Exchange Act. Of course, the market information from foreign exchanges is widely available in the U.S. Thus, the restrictions on foreign screens essentially limit foreign exchanges from admitting U.S. persons as members. The only exception to this rule was a small volume exception granted in 1999 for Tradepoint Financial Networks plc, which operates as a securities exchange from facilities in London as the Tradepoint Stock Exchange. The SEC made the exemption effective with certain conditions:

- The average daily dollar value of trades (measured on a quarterly basis) involving a U.S. member may not exceed $40 million; and its worldwide average daily volume (measured on a quarterly basis) does not exceed ten percent of the average daily volume of the LSE.

- In addition, the screens displaying quotations in securities not registered under the Exchange Act may be accessible only to qualified institutional buyers or QIBs (generally defined in Rule 144A as an entity that owns and invests on a discretionary basis at least $100 million in securities of unaffiliated issuers), non-U.S. persons, and international agencies. The unregistered securities may be resold only through the Tradepoint QIB Market or otherwise outside the U.S.

The last group of players is the brokers. Again, a broker-dealer generally cannot do business with U.S. investors unless it registers as a broker-dealer under section 15 of the Exchange Act. Section 3(a)(4) of the Exchange Act defines a broker generally as any person engaged in the business of effecting transactions in securities for the account of others. Section 3(a)(5) of the Exchange Act defines a "dealer" generally as a person that is "engaged in the business of buying and selling securities" for its own account through a broker or otherwise, and excepts persons who do not buy or sell securities "as part of a regular business."

Registered broker-dealers are subject to U.S. laws, regulations and supervisory structures intended to protect investors and the securities markets. Before it begins doing business, a broker-dealer must become a member of an SRO.

This registration allows the SEC and SROs, for example, to review qualifications of a broker-dealer or to properly examine a broker-dealer. It also is designed to assure that broker-dealers maintain adequate competency levels, by satisfying SRO qualification requirements. The registration and other SEC and SRO requirements allow investors to learn about the professional background, registration/license statuses and conduct of registered broker-dealers.

In addition, every registered broker-dealer must be a member of the Securities Investor Protection Corporation, or SIPC, which was created by Congress to provide a mechanism to assist customers of a registered broker-dealer in receiving their cash and securities up to specified limits in the event of liquidation by the broker-dealer.

Broker-dealers are subject to statutory disqualification standards and the SEC's and SRO's disciplinary authority, which are designed to prevent persons with an adverse disciplinary history from becoming, or becoming associated with, registered broker-dealers. Broker-dealers also are subject to financial responsibility requirements that are designed to safeguard customer assets.

Broker-dealers must meet certain financial responsibility requirements, including: maintaining minimum amounts of liquid assets, or net capital; safeguarding the customer funds and securities; and making and preserving accurate books and records.

Broker-dealers are subject to extensive sales practice standards under federal laws and SRO rules. Antifraud provisions of the securities laws prohibit misstatements or misleading omissions of material facts, and fraudulent or manipulative acts and practices. Broker-dealers owe their customers a duty of fair dealing. They must seek to obtain best execution, that is, the most favorable terms available under the circumstances, for their customer orders. They must only make suitable recommendations. They must disclose all known material facts to investors before effecting a trade. A broker-dealer must provide its customers, at or before the completion of a transaction, with basic information about the trade. To prevent insider trading, Section

15(f) of the Act specifically requires broker-dealers to have and enforce written policies and procedures reasonably designed to prevent their employees from misusing material non-public information.

The reason for these essential provisions is investor protection and the financial soundness of the securities markets.

While, generally, foreign broker-dealers dealing with U.S. customers in the U.S. must register with the SEC, seventeen years ago, the SEC exempted foreign broker-dealers from registration in certain circumstances. The SEC said in Rule 15-a6 that a foreign broker can do business with U.S. investors and brokers without registration within certain conditions, including

(1) execution of unsolicited securities transactions;

   _**or**_

(2) solicited contacts limited to:

   (a) providing research reports to large institutional investors;

   (b) effecting transactions for large institutional investors, if the trade is booked through a US-registered broker or dealer; or

   (3) executing transactions directly with U.S. registered brokers or dealers.

The most direct forms of contact under the rule are limited to "major U.S. institutional investors" which are functionally similar to QIBs. The rationale for limiting these types of direct contracts to QIB-like-entities is based on the limited ability of smaller investors, especially individuals, to marshal the necessary resources or investment expertise to fully assess the risks of transacting with foreign broker-dealers without the intermediation of a U.S. broker-dealer. These investors may not recognize the implications of transacting directly with a foreign broker-dealer including difficulty in (i) determining their ability to obtain redress for botched transactions, (ii) understanding the screening process for agents of the foreign broker-dealer, and (iii) understanding the different conduct standards that apply to the foreign broker-dealer.

For example, to become licensed to sell securities, all persons associated with a U.S. broker-dealer are required to pass a qualifications test covering substantive aspects of the securities business. SEC and SRO rules also are designed to assure that those persons associated with broker-dealers who have committed abuses that would make them subject to a statutory disqualification are prohibited from working in the securities industry or are subject to appropriate conditions such as enhanced supervision. The SROs also require that persons involved in the management of the broker-dealer pass additional examinations relating to supervisory procedures and requirements. These qualification requirements are supplemented by continuing education requirements, the broker-dealer's duty to supervise its employees to prevent violations of the federal securities laws, and the specific supervisory procedures imposed by the SROs. In addition, our rules and those of the SROs provide firms with targeted sales practice standards to address particular types of abuse. Furthermore, U.S. broker-dealers and their associated persons must comply with specific guidelines concerning the content and review of communications with the public, including advertisements. Smaller investors transacting more directly with foreign broker-dealers may lack the ability to effectively assess what, if any, similar protections are afforded under a different regulatory regime.

The requirement that foreign brokers be registered in order to directly contact US individuals and small institutions is wholly consistent with the registration requirements for US broker-dealers. US broker-dealers must be registered to deal with all investors, large and small, and the broker-dealer investor protection standards apply to their dealings with all investors, with a few exceptions for large institutions. In contrast, unregistered securities can be sold to individuals that are "accredited investors," and hedge funds can be sold to unlimited numbers of individuals that are "qualified purchasers." Why is that?

First, it must be recognized that broker-dealer regulation is a predicate for the unregistered security and hedge fund exceptions. In most cases, these products are sold by broker-dealers to investors, who are more dependent on the broker-dealer's advice, given the lack of standardized disclosures or investment restrictions for these products. It has long been acknowledged that most investors rely heavily on the advice of their advisors even when they have full disclosure documents. As the SEC's Special Study of Securities Markets said in 1963, "No amount of disclosure in a prospectus can be effective to protect investors unless the securities are sold by a salesman who understands and appreciates both the nature of the securities he sells and his responsibilities to the investor to whom he sells." So in these cases, regulation of broker-dealers is especially important.

In addition, while wealth can enable individual investors to spread their risk through diversification, or allow them to sustain some losses without dramatic changes to their living standard, some may argue that it is not a reliable standard of sophistication for individuals dealing with a broker-dealer. The securities markets are replete with examples of wealthy investors being misled or defrauded by firms hawking securities. And securities firms that cater to affluent individuals readily admit that wealth is not always a reliable proxy for sophistication in dealing with financial advisors. Individual wealth can be attained in many ways, some of which develop sophistication in financial matters, but many of which don't. In contrast, large institutions have the structure and the resources to hire dedicated staff that can develop sophistication in financial matters. For these reason, the SEC has consistently required broker-dealer registration for all US brokers dealing with US investors, and has applied US customer protection standards to their dealings with all but the largest institutional investors, even when they were selling unregistered securities.

At the same time as it adopted Rule 15a-6, the SEC published a concept release on the concept of recognizing foreign country regulation of broker-dealers in place of U.S. registration. The practical effect of current law is that foreign exchanges and foreign broker-dealers dealing directly with U.S. investors in the United States must either register or be exempt from registration.

While registration is considered by critics as onerous, the exemption has also essentially required that firms that want to regularly provide services to U.S. customers establish a U.S. broker-dealer affiliate to interface with those customers. Some have criticized this regulation as economic protectionism designed to preserve the position of U.S. financial services provides and markets.

Today: The Pressures
You may ask, how all of this working in practice? I would answer that while U.S. regulation is providing valuable protection to U.S. investors, this approach to registration of foreign markets and broker-dealers could benefit from consideration of developments in today's capital markets.

For example, can you, as an individual, own interest in an E.U. company, XYZ Company, today? The answer is yes, and it can be done many ways. You can buy a mutual fund or an ETF with a large stake in XYZ Co., obtaining the benefit of the expertise and acumen of the mutual fund adviser. You can buy XYZ Co. American Depository Receipts under certain ADR programs. You could buy XYZ Co. ordinary shares from your broker who may sell it out of inventory, or buy it from U.S. market makers in XYZ Co. Or, the U.S. broker may buy the shares on a foreign exchange though a foreign affiliate that is a member of that exchange or though a non-affiliate correspondent broker-dealer.

Thus, if the SEC's investor protection concern is about retail access to unregistered securities, it is already here. For instance, a major U.S. on-line broker-dealer recently announced its new global trading platform, which will allow individual-investor customers in the U.S. to buy and sell foreign securities in their local currency. The firm is starting with online trading for stocks in Canada, France, Germany, Hong Kong, Japan and the United Kingdom, but it also is offering broker-assisted trading in additional countries and hopes to eventually include as many as 42 international markets and related currencies in the online system. I suspect that other U.S. broker-dealers have or are developing similar foreign trading systems.

With regard to institutional investors generally, the largest ones maintain foreign trading desks in places like Tokyo, Hong Kong, London, and Paris. They access foreign exchanges though foreign broker-dealers without any involvement of U.S. broker-dealers. Other large institutions access foreign markets to buy foreign securities through a foreign broker operating under Rule 15a-6, with the trade being booked through a U.S. broker-dealer. Other institutions trade in foreign markets through U.S. brokers, who execute in foreign markets electronically through affiliates.

As retail ownership of securities has increased since the 1980s, so, too, has investment activity in foreign securities. U.S. gross transactions in foreign securities grew dramatically from $53 billion to almost $7.4 trillion since the 1980s. Nearly two-thirds of all equity investors in 2005 hold foreign equities through ownership of individual stock in foreign companies or ownership of international or global mutual funds, up from about half in 1999 and 2002.

Many experts advise investors, for diversification reasons, to have international investments in their portfolios. This is true despite questions about investor protection and issue disclosure arrangements in some foreign markets. We recognize the broad economic benefits that can be gained for incorporating foreign securities into an individual's portfolio. However, an advisor generally serve as a gatekeeper and performs due diligence, when retail investors purchase foreign securities through directed brokerage plans or through mutual funds. As more sophisticated parties, advisors generally are in a better position to understand the differences between regulatory regimes and make appropriate decisions.

To reprise the current situation, US investors have a growing appetite for foreign securities, which they are obtaining in various ways. Individuals purchasing foreign securities are currently doing so through US brokers or investment advisers, and thus are protected by US regulation of the brokers' or advisers' conduct. US institutions may have greater contact with foreign brokers, but to the extent they are trading from within the US, the foreign broker's activities are still limited by the conditions of Rule 15a-6. US brokers access foreign exchanges through foreign brokers.

Over the years, a number of foreign markets and jurisdictions have questioned whether registration of foreign markets and brokers in the US is essential to investor protection if the foreign jurisdiction affords regulation comparable to that in the US. European Union countries in particular have been complaining that the U.S. "pro-investor protection" stand is protectionist of our domestic institutions and firms.

The SEC's response has generally been that our statutory mandate requires us to place investor protection first, and we currently provide better than national treatment to foreign entities, who are welcome to do business here if they register, or for brokers, if they comply with the significantly less demanding terms of Rule 15a-6. Frankly, I can't agree with suggestions that our prudential regulatory requirements are protectionist-motivated, or that investors are denied fundamental access to foreign securities or markets.

However, there may be more that we can do to reduce costs and frictions of obtaining foreign securities in the US, without jeopardizing investor protection for US investors. In fact, we may be able to work cooperatively with foreign regulators to raise standards for investors in all of our markets.

A Cooperative Approach
In thinking about a cooperative approach, it would not be my aim to forego all protections, enabling foreign exchanges and foreign broker-dealers to conduct business within U.S. borders without any conditions or regulation. This approach may be inconsistent with the SEC's legal obligations and would erode the investor protections that have contributed to the preeminence of the U.S. financial markets. In fact, the integrity of the U.S. system likely would be jeopardized: facing competition from lightly regulated foreign firms, U.S. financial services providers may choose to relocate overseas.

We need a different solution.

The SEC has broad general exemptive authority, provided it can make findings with regard to the public interest and the protection of investors. In 1996, Congress provided the SEC with flexibility to regulate the marketplace by giving the SEC broad authority to exempt any person from any of the provisions of the Exchange Act and impose appropriate conditions on their operation. The Exchange Act was enacted at a time when it was recognized that a regulatory structure for securities exchanges would "be of little value tomorrow if it is not flexible enough to meet new conditions immediately as they arise and demand attention in the public interest." As the Senate recognized in 1934, "exchanges cannot be regulated efficiently under a rigid statutory program....considerable latitude is allowed for the exercise of administrative discretion in the regulation of both exchanges and the over-the-counter market."[16] Those statements ring evermore true today. The SEC's exemptive authority, combined with the ability to facilitate a national market system, provides the SEC with the tools it needs to adopt a cooperative framework without compromising its mandate of investor protection.

The SEC would therefore need to make a determination that it is in the public interest, and consistent with the protection of investors, if foreign exchanges and broker-dealers are to be exempted from portions of the federal securities laws.

On what basis might we come to this conclusion?

First, foreign exchange screens in the United States -

As I discussed earlier, under the Exchange Act, exchanges can only admit brokers as members. Investors access exchanges through regulated brokers. Few, if any, foreign exchanges admit non-brokers as members, and I see little reason to change this fundamental approach.

As I also discussed earlier, information from foreign exchanges is widely available now. So the key issue is U.S. broker membership in U.S. foreign exchanges. Foreign exchanges can differ dramatically in their structure, acceptable trading practices, and oversight from U.S. markets.

So a new cooperative approach could offer the possibility of U.S. brokers joining foreign exchanges in jurisdictions with exchange regulation and oversight standards comparable to the U.S. where the jurisdiction cooperates with the SEC in assuring investor protection, as well as other statutory requirements.

Under this cooperation approach, the SEC could establish by rule conditions for exemption of exchange registration to foreign exchanges from jurisdictions that satisfy the conditions. Material breaches of any of the conditions would be grounds for the SEC to withdraw the exemption from a foreign exchange.

What conditions would be appropriate?

Recognized Jurisdiction - The foreign exchange should be subject to regulatory oversight in its primary jurisdiction that protects investors and the integrity of the securities markets, including that which addresses: fair markets; fraud; manipulation; insider trading; current trade reporting; net capital and financial responsibility of exchange members; and surveillance and enforcement. In addition, as a measure of comity, the foreign jurisdiction should provide regulatory relief to U.S. exchanges seeking to conduct business in that jurisdiction that is at least as extensive as that provided by the SEC.

__Notice to Investors__ - Investors should have notice that their trading is being done in a foreign marketplace, which may not offer the same protections afforded to them in the United States. As discussed earlier, advancements in technology have made the physical location of an exchange an elusive concept. Given what is at stake, it is imperative that investors chose the foreign marketplace knowingly, and with full disclosure of the relevant differences.

__Foreign Securities Only__ - In my view, the need for exemption is limited to access to foreign securities, rather than U.S.-registered issues. These are the securities sought overseas by U.S. investors. Moreover, the advantages this cooperative approach would give unregistered foreign exchanges over U.S. registered exchanges are hardest to justify with respect to U.S. securities. "Foreign securities" while hard to define, would look both at the nature of the issue and the U.S. share of trading volume.

__U.S. Membership Limited to Broker-Dealers__ - As I mentioned, the foreign exchange should not provide direct access to U.S. persons other than registered U.S. broker-dealers.

__Fair Access__ - And, it would not be appropriate for an exempt foreign exchange to unfairly discriminate among U.S. broker-dealers or U.S. and foreign broker-dealers in granting access to services. To allow foreign exchanges to discriminate unfairly would call into question the purpose of the exemption.

__MOU__ - It would be important that the SEC and the non-US exchange's home regulator coordinate their oversight in a manner designed to assure effective regulation in both jurisdictions. Among other things, the SEC and the foreign regulator should coordinate inspections, and regularly share information regarding the exchange. This goal may be accomplished through memoranda of understanding with the foreign regulator that address information sharing and other forms of regulatory cooperation.

Recordkeeping, Reporting and Disclosure - I would want for the SEC to be able to obtain access to separately identifiable audit trail of orders sent to, and executed on, the foreign exchange by U.S. members. The SEC should also have access to trading information involving U.S. investors. I would also want to ensure that any privacy laws in an exchange's home country would not impede its ability to provide the SEC with books and records relating to the U.S. activities of the foreign exchange.

Among other major consequences, this cooperative approach would avoid the foreign exchange from needing to file its changes in rules for approval by the SEC. U.S. exchanges still must do so. Clearly, this disparity would be noticed by U.S. exchanges. To relieve this competitive disadvantage, the SEC would need to consider speeding up the rule filing process for trading rules.

With regard to foreign broker-dealers, a similar cooperative approach could apply to foreign brokers dealing with large institutional investors. In effect, this would ease the requirements of Rule 15a-6 for foreign brokers subject to comparable regulation by their host jurisdiction, allowing them to deal directly U.S. QIBs in the U.S. I am mindful that if not carefully structured, this approach could raise investor protection concerns, as well as competitive concerns for U.S. brokers. With certain parameters, however, those concerns may be minimized.

In order to preserve investor protection and promote market competition, this cooperative approach for foreign brokers would depend on a determination that the home country regulatory regime for brokers dealing with overseas clients is comparable to the protections provided to US investors by US broker-dealer oversight. At least initially, I would envision it being limited to encompassing transactions in which a foreign broker-dealer deals with U.S. QIBs in the U.S. in foreign securities or U.S. government securities.

Limiting the transactions to foreign securities focuses the approach on where the need for direct access to foreign brokers is most compelling: access to foreign securities. U.S. investors are likely to have a greater expectation that transactions involving domestic securities (as opposed to foreign securities) will be subject to full SEC oversight. The limitation to QIBs, at least initially, helps ensure that the investors involved are familiar with foreign market practices, and have the resources to understand and bear the risks of dealing with an unregistered foreign broker-dealer. It also reflects the inherent imprecision in comparing U.S. and home country supervision of broker-dealers.

Finally, recognition of foreign broker-dealer registration and regulators as substantively equivalent to U.S. broker-dealer registration and regulators could be conditioned on further basic requirements:

(A) the existence of a supervisory cooperation, investigative and financial memorandum of understanding between the SEC and the foreign regulatory authority;

(B) compliance by foreign broker-dealers with specific U.S. regulatory requirements including notice and record access requirements; and

(C) reciprocal treatment of U.S. broker-dealers by the home jurisdiction of the foreign broker-dealer.

Conclusion

While the SEC raised the concept of mutual recognition for brokers 17 years ago, it still is a novel approach for it. In thinking it through, the SEC needs to be deliberate, for much is at stake. The SEC also needs to think about how investors are informed about the destination of their orders given the many ways that an order for foreign securities can be executed as the world becomes more closely linked. But there is much to be gained from a cooperative approach. Through greater communication and cooperation between international regulators and comparison of regulatory regimes, a degree of harmonization may result that produces stronger protections for investors in many jurisdictions. At the same time, this approach offers the promise of reducing the costs of trading around the globe.

INDEX

McLaren Legal Publishers

For a full catalog,

please visit our website at:

www.mclarenpublishing.com